Intelligent Guides to Wines & Top Vineyards

Tuscany

Chianti, Montalcino, and Bolgheri

June 2018 edition

Wines of Tuscany
ISBN: 9781980411093
Benjamin Lewin MW
Copyright © 2016, 2017, 2018 Benjamin Lewin
Vendange Press
www.vendangepress.com

D0043035

Preface

This guide to the wines of Tuscany covers the trend-setting regions: Bolgheri, Montalcino, and Chianti Classico. The first part of the guide discusses the regions, and explains the character and range of the wines. The second part profiles the producers. There are detailed profiles of the leading producers, showing how each winemaker interprets the local character, and mini-profiles of other important estates.

In the first part, I address the nature of the wines made today and ask how this has changed, how it's driven by tradition or competition, and how styles may evolve in the future. I show how the wines are related to the terroir and to the types of grape varieties that are grown, and I explain the classification system. For each region, I suggest reference wines that illustrate the character and variety of the area.

In the second part, there's no single definition for what constitutes a top producer. Leading producers range from those who are so prominent as to represent the common public face of an appellation to those who demonstrate an unexpected potential on a tiny scale. The producers profiled in the guide represent the best of both tradition and innovation in wine in the region. In each profile, I have tried to give a sense of the producer's aims for his wines, of the personality and philosophy behind them—to meet the person who makes the wine, as it were, as much as to review the wines themselves.

Each profile shows a sample label, a picture of the winery, and details of production, followed by a description of the producer and winemaker. Each producer is rated (from one to three stars). For each producer I suggest reference wines that are a good starting point for understanding the style. Most of the producers welcome visits, although some require appointments: details are in the profiles. Profiles are organized geographically, and each group of profiles is preceded by maps showing the locations of producers to help plan itineraries.

The guide is based on visits to Tuscany over recent years. I owe an enormous debt to the producers who cooperated in this venture by engaging in discussion and opening innumerable bottles for tasting. This guide would not have been possible without them.

Benjamin Lewin

Contents

Tables

Appellation Maps

Producer Maps

Overview of Italy

Is it unfair to say that the regulation of wine production in Italy is in permanent disorder? Having copied the French system, with wine divided into Vino da Tavola (table wine), IGT (Indicazione Geografica Tipica, now officially renamed as IGP), and the quality wine levels of DOC (Denominazione di Origine Controllata) and DOCG (a super-DOC category), Italy finds itself in the topsy-turvy situation that in some regions its best wines are labeled as IGTs rather than DOCGs. DOC and DOCG both officially have been replaced by DOP [Denominazione di Origine Protetta], but in true Italian fashion no one is paying much attention to the latest European regulations.

Long and skinny, extending over 10 degrees of latitude from north to south, Italy offers more diversity of climates than any other European wine producer, from cool climate Trentino-Alto-Adige in the far north, to beating hot Sicily in the far south. Italy also has an unusually high number of indigenous grape varieties. Plantings of black varieties are slightly ahead of white overall. The top red wines come from the Nebbiolo grape in Piedmont and the Sangiovese grape in Tuscany, neither of which is grown successfully anywhere else. It's fair to say that, while Italy has many distinguished red wines, it's relatively hard to find an interesting white wine.

Italy plays tag with France for the title of the world's largest wine producer and exporter. The proportion of quality wine has been increasing, up from 13% in 1988 to 30% today, but that still leaves table wine as the major part of wine production. The relative increase in quality wine is mostly due to the fact that table wine production is declining more rapidly than other categories. About two thirds of the DOC(G) regions, and the majority of quality wine production, are in the northern half of the country. Production in the South has declined significantly in the past decade.

There are 74 DOCGs and 334 DOCs. Most of the DOCGs have staked out an identify and are reasonably well known. Without the same imprimatur of quality, DOCs are rather more variable. There are 118 IGTs, which is far too many for wines that should have a broader geographical range and diversity of character. Failure of the DOCGs to keep up with modern trends (such as the exclusion of traditional varieties that lower quality) means that the situation in Tuscany, where many top wines are not part of the DOCG system, has extended elsewhere.

All regions of Italy produce both red and white wine. The most common variety in each region is usually indigenous, although international varieties are making some headway here as everywhere else. This is especially true in Tuscany.

The Ranks of Tuscany

Tuscany is Italy's most important wine region in terms of the combination of quality and diversity, offering a range of styles extending from the lively freshness of Sangiovese in Chianti Classico to the sterner character of Sangiovese in Brunello di Montalcino, chocolaty from a modernist, deliciously savory from a traditionalist, to the international styles of Bolgheri based mostly on Bordeaux varieties. And from all these areas as well as others come the completely undefined category of the so-called "super-Tuscans."

In Tuscany, reality is so far distant from the DOC system that many of the very best wines are super-Tuscans—basically wines that may use indigenous varieties or focus on "international" varieties, that may or may not actually meet the criteria for the local DOC, but that are sold under the IGT Toscana label, although IGT is nominally lower in the level of classification than DOC(G). Indeed, producers often feel compelled to have an IGT Toscana to maintain credibility, and their top wines are likely to be IGT rather than DOC. Nowhere else in Italy has the system of classification been so turned upside down.

All the regions have a hierarchy within the DOC system. In Bolgheri, the distinction is between Bolgheri plain and simple, and Bolgheri Superiore. In Chianti Classico and Montalcino, Riserva indicates a higher level based simply on longer aging. Montalcino also has a lower level called Rosso, while Chianti Classico has a higher one called Gran Selezione. In each case, the basic difference between levels in the hierarchy is that higher levels require longer aging, sometimes with a minimum time in wood, but there aren't usually any other specifications that relate directly to quality.

In Chianti Classico and Montalcino there has been something of a transition from making the top wines based on selection to focusing on individual vineyards. Formerly the best wines were based on selection of lots for more extended aging under the Riserva classification. Today producers often talk about their "Crus," meaning top vineyards that would be classified as Premier or Grand Cru if such a system existed. Sometimes these are described as Vigna or Vigneto followed by the name of the vineyard. The wines are often found at the highest classification in the local DOC system, but the name has more prominence than the classification.

The hilly terrain of Tuscany is covered in vineyards, olive groves, and forests. Many wine producers also make olive oil, although I have found scarcely any who will admit to making a profit on the olive oil; it's claimed to be more a traditional accompaniment to wine production than a profit center. It used to be said that vineyards were planted on land that could not be used to grow anything else; and olive trees were planted where you could not even grow grapevines. "Chianti was a survival econ-

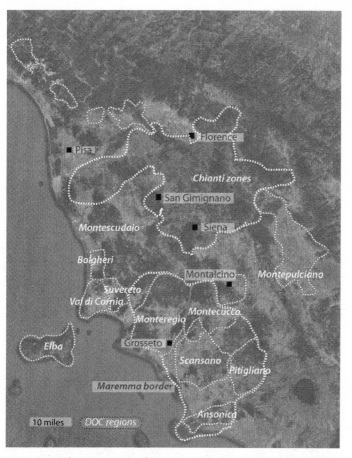

Wine is made over much of Tuscany. There are about 30 DOCs and DOCGs. The most important are named.

omy until the 1950s or 60s," says Giuseppe Mazzocolin of Felsina. Most farms practiced polyculture, and the focus on viticulture is really a matter of the past two or three decades.

Talk of the "rolling hills of Tuscany" is romantic twaddle; except for the coastal regions of Maremma and Bolgheri, most of the best vineyards are on relatively steep and abrupt hillsides. Driving around to visit wineries, you find many located well off the beaten track, often on unpaved roads winding up steep hillsides. The relationships between vineyards are not always obvious. I remember taking a wrong turn on my first visit to Querciabella: more or less at the top of the mountain, I asked a local where it was, and he said, "Just there," pointing across the valley to a more or less equivalent point on the opposite side, several miles back down and

The Indigenous Grapes of Tuscany

Sangiovese is a noble variety by any measure, relatively light in color, with high natural acidity, and a tendency to savory flavors on the palate.

Canaiolo was important in the nineteenth century, bringing greater body and ripeness (and alcohol) to the blend in Chianti.

Colorino is deeply colored and was used to bring color to Chianti, but is much less used today because of its lack of flavor intensity.

Ciliegiolo gives light red cherry flavors; it has fallen out of favor because it is difficult to grow.

Pugnitello fell out of favor because of its very low yields, but some wineries have reintroduced it for its intense flavor and spiciness.

Mammolo is a somewhat perfumed black variety that is no longer much used in the Chianti blend.

Malvasia Nera is a black variety of Malvasia, which may be the same as Tempranillo, but is not often seen today.

Malvasia is a white grape that is no longer allowed in the Chianti blend, but is used for Vin Santo dessert wine.

Trebbiano is grown in Tuscany (as everywhere in Italy) but is no longer allowed in Chianti, although it can be used for the Vin Santo dessert wine.

Moscadella is a fairly nondescript white variety that is used to make slightly sparking sweet wines.

then up again. Often built into hillsides or underground, wineries may be much larger than they appear. Olive groves are usually interspersed with the vineyards. Tuscany has about 86,000 ha of vineyards, of which 30,000 are classified as DOC or DOCG.

Savage Sangiovese

"Sangiovese, Nebbiolo, and Pinot Noir are the three worst grapes in the world—to make the three best wines," says Francesco Ripaccioli at Canalicchio di Sopra in Montalcino. Widely grown, Sangiovese is Italy's most important black grape variety, regarded as a workhouse grape all over the southern part of the country. (It's also grown on Corsica, where it is called Nielluccio.) It is in Tuscany, however, where it can claim to be a noble variety, making great wines that reflect individual terroirs.

The traditional red wines of Tuscany all are based on Sangiovese: the major regions are Brunello di Montalcino, Chianti, and Vino Nobile de Montepulciano. Brunello di Montalcino insists on 100% Sangiovese (of which more later); the other regions allow other varieties to be blended with the Sangiovese. Chianti looms over everything else; altogether it accounts for about half of the DOC(G) vineyards and produces 8 million cases of wine each year. Chianti's best area, Chianti Classico DOCG, is quite distinct, and should not be confused with other Chianti DOCGs. Vino Nobile de Montepulciano (there is no connection with the Montepulciano grape) is roughly comparable in quality to the outlying Chianti DOCs.

Sangiovese is a variety with considerable diversity. For a long time, Brunello di Montalcino was considered to have an advantage in quality over Chianti because of the cultivars being planted. When Sangiovese was introduced into Montalcino, producer Biondi-Santi identified a clone of Sangiovese in his vineyards, which he named Brunello (the little brown one). Sangiovese Grosso is used to describe a family of clones that evolved from the Biondi-Santi's original clone. Descendants of this strain still are prominent in Montalcino, although there is very extensive clonal variation in Sangiovese, and now hundreds of different clones have been identified. The other general strain is called Sangiovese Piccolo, and this was more common in Chianti.

Perhaps the main difference in Chianti over the past twenty years has been the improvement in the quality of the Sangiovese. From the 1960s, most plantings used a clone of Sangiovese (R10) that was too productive, giving wines with simple structure and limited aging potential. Since the 1990s, extensive research has led to the development of better clones, with smaller, better spaced berries on smaller bunches, leading to much higher quality wine with good structure, better color, and more interesting aromatics. Several wineries in Montalcino and Chianti have actively been developing clones suited to their particular terroirs, and the Chianti Classico 2000 project, supported by the Consorzio, spent 16 years testing clones in experimental vineyards. With the development of new clones, the supposed difference between Sangiovese Grosso and Piccolo has become insignificant.

One interesting result of all this is that the supposed advantage of Montalcino in having higher quality Sangiovese has become no more than a myth; in fact, the best clones in Montalcino, including Biondi-Santi's fabled BBS11, do not necessarily do so well in Chianti. Sangiovese somewhat resembles Riesling in the way its performance reflects terroir. As Guido Orzalesi of the Altesino winery in Montalcino ruefully noted, when they tried propagating vines from their famous Montosoli vineyard in other locations, the results did not give the very special qualities of Montosoli. It took 25 years to eliminate the terrible R10 clone from Chianti, but now much of the Classico region is planted with high quality clones; certainly there is no excuse for poor results.

Sangiovese was traditionally aged in botti (large casks of 20-60 hl) made from Slavonian oak (at back), but barriques (225 liters) or tonneaux (500 liters) of French oak (at front) are now also used to help tame the tannins.

Sangiovese is naturally a lightly colored variety; the idea of making more deeply colored wine created an impetus to blend it with other varieties. Increased fruit concentration coming from the new clones takes off some of the pressure to ameliorate the nature of the grape, although Sangiovese is not a variety that benefits from excessive extraction. "Applying the concept of phenolic ripeness to Sangiovese is like the tail wagging the dog," says Francesco Cinzano of Col d'Orcia in Montalcino. The motto for Sangiovese should be "never too much," says Giuseppe Mazzocolin of Fattoria di Felsina in Chianti.

The tradition in Tuscany, in both Chianti Classico and Montalcino, is to age wine in large casks of Slavonian oak. The traditional shape for these botti is oval, but sometimes they are circular. They vary from 30 hl to 100 hl. Sometimes producers change to Austrian or French oak, and, of course, barriques of French oak are now found; as the barrique is 225 liters (or just over 2 hl), its use implies a significantly greater exposure to oak. In Montalcino, all DOC wine must be 100% Sangiovese, but in Chianti Classico, upto 20% can be other varieties, including international varieties as well as the old indigenous varieties. It might seem that whether a producer is to be regarded as traditionalist or modernist could be assessed by the use of botti versus barriques and (in Chianti Classico) by whether international varieties are included, but it is not always so simple, although it is true that wines tend to have a smoother impression moving more towards black fruits when barriques are used, and a darker color with more impression of structure when international varieties are used in Chianti Classico.

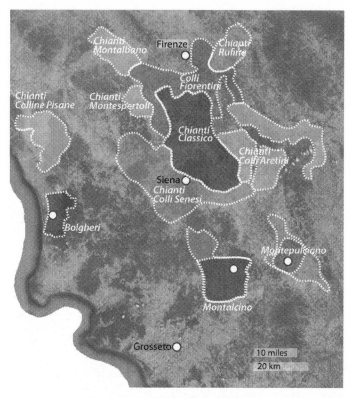

Major DOCs of Tuscany include Chianti Classico (center) and the Chianti subareas (surrounding Chianti Classico). The most important region for Sangiovese is Montalcino (dark: farther south). Montepulciano (to the east) also grows Sangiovese. Bolgheri is home to several super-Tuscans.

Sangiovese is a reductive variety, which is to say that its aroma and flavor spectrum are more affected than most by exposure to oxygen. It's not only the tannins that are changed by the aging regime, but also the aromatic profile. The characteristic organoleptic spectrum of Sangiovese, especially as aged in botti, has faintly savage, animal overtones, definitely savory, sometimes a mineral hint of gunflint. Aging in barriques suppresses those savory notes and brings out more direct fruits, perhaps as a result of greater oxidative exposure. So what's the true typicity (or tipicità as they would have it in Italy) of Sangiovese?

The Hills of Chianti

Chianti dominates wine production in Tuscany, although there is a significant difference between the Chianti Classico DOCG (the heart of the

Tuscan wine estates usually have olive trees planted next to vineyards.

old region) and the other seven Chianti DOCGs. The Classico area extends around a line between Florence and Siena; this was where Chianti gained its original reputation, and obtained the right to the description Chianti Classico in 1932. But a variety of surrounding areas also gained the right to use Chianti, with individual zonal descriptions, beginning the general degeneration of its meaning. There was a protracted legal fight about the right to use "Chianti," which the Chianti Classico producers essentially lost. Even worse, Chianti, with no qualification, can be used by a variety of areas elsewhere in Tuscany that have no real connection with Chianti per se.

It is probably a lost cause to point out that Chianti Classico is a separate DOCG, quite distinct from Chianti DOCG, which is divided into seven areas. Part of the reason is that where Chianti extends into quality regions, most notably where Chianti Colli Senesi to the south includes Montalcino and Montepulciano, all wines with pretension to quality have the right to the more restricted local DOCG name. The only unifying aspect is that all the areas of Chianti, like Chianti Classico, are dominated by Sangiovese. So are other parts of Tuscany, such as Vino Nobile di Montepulciano, and no one confuses them with Chianti Classico. But the fact that Chianti Classico is not merely one part of "Chianti," but is an independent region is not well understood.

The only one of the other Chiantis to have any pretension to the same quality as Chianti Classico is Chianti Rufina, just to the northeast. Rufina is the smallest zone in Chianti, the farthest from the sea, with vineyards

A pile of straw-covered bottles reflects history, but has little to do with Chianti of today.

mostly above 500m, and has a more Continental climate. Chianti Rufina must have more than 70% Sangiovese, which allows for a lot of variation. The top wines age well—I have had lovely examples more than 25 years old—but the wine can be on the sturdy side when young. In a word, it is rarely as refined as Chianti Classico.

Chianti Classico has been struggling to establish its reputation as a quality wine region. And it took a long time to recover from the post-second world war image of wine in a straw covered bottle. The bottle was certainly more interesting than the wine. But slowly Chianti became a serious wine. Chianti today is a mix of artisanal and large-scale production. Half of the several hundred members of the Chianti Classico Consorzio bottle their own wine; vineyard holdings vary from as little as 1 ha to as much as 200 ha. The largest single producer is the cooperative Castelli del Grevepesa, which represents 160 growers; Antinori, Frescobaldi, Ruffino, and Barone Ricasoli are all major producers.

Although Chianti was one of the better known wines of Italy a century ago, to the point at which there was a problem with fraudulent imitations, it has developed slowly in the past half century. In the 1960s, it was regarded as uneconomic for wine production because of the hilly terrain. Luca di Napoli at Castello dei Rampolla recollects that making wine was not easy. "People bought sugar and brought in wine from elsewhere—it was a black economy. The role of the oenologue was to be the link to buy the wine from the south."

Chianti's history speaks to the issues in winemaking with Sangiovese. The driving factor has always been the need to tame the tannins, typically accentuated by high acidity, whether this has led to blending with other varieties or the use of barriques instead of botti.

Changing Regulations Have Made Chianti Classico a Quality Wine

	Sangiovese	Colorino Canaiolo	Malvasia Trebbiano	Other varieties
1967	less than 70%	maximum 20%	minimum 10%	15% grapes permitted from other regions!
1984	minimum 75%	maximum 10%	minimum 2%	10% of international varieties allowed
1996	minimum 80% maximum 100%		maximum 6%	limit increased to 15%
2000				limit increased to 20%
2006			banned	

Chianti started as a blended wine. The problem was that the original blend created an issue with quality. Chianti as we know it today had its origins in 1872, when Baron Ricasoli (a future Prime Minister of Italy) recommended a blend of 70% Sangiovese, 15% Canaiolo and 15% Malvasia. This formula was followed when the first DOC regulations came into effect in 1967. The rationale was that Canaiolo (an undistinguished black variety) bulked out the wine and improved the color, while including the white Malvasia softened the harsh tannins. Colorino (a grape with colored pulp but little taste) was also used to bump up the color. Chianti has changed a lot since then. Slowly the requirements for including low quality indigenous varieties, including white grapes, were reduced. International varieties were allowed in small quantities, which were later increased. Finally white grapes were banned, and monovarietal Sangiovese was allowed.

These changes reflect the status of Sangiovese. Improved viticulture gave more reliable ripening and better color, so the inclusion of Colorino, with its dilution of taste, became undesirable. Better methods of vinification gave riper tannins, making it unnecessary to include white grapes. Even so, the over-productive varieties of the eighties did not have enough structure, so producers decided that they could best improve their Sangiovese by including more structured varieties, such as Cabernet Sauvignon. Merlot is sometimes used to give a more generous impression. "In the eighties when we understood we had to improve the quality, a lot of wineries felt they had to use international varieties because it was difficult to reliably produce high quality with Sangiovese," says Sergio Zingarelli, president of the Consorzio.

Types of Wine in Chianti Classico

Chianti Classico	At least 80% Sangiovese, minimum alcohol 12%, aging for one year (method unspecified).
Riserva	Minimum alcohol 12.5%, aging for 2 years, including 3 months in bottle.
Gran Selezione	Minimum alcohol 13%, aging for 30 months, including 3 months in bottle.
Vigna or Vigneto	The name following Vigna or Vigneto is the name of a single vineyard. Usually used for vineyards that producers consider to be equivalent to Crus, but no legal definition.
Vin Santo	Made from dried Trebbiano and Malvasia grapes: sweet with high alcohol. Aging lasts 3-8 years in very small casks.

Finally the Sangiovese reached a quality level at which many producers feel they can make a one hundred percent Sangiovese that has sufficient quality in its aroma and flavor spectrum so as not to need any other grapes. "With Chianti Classico 2000, we found several clones that are high quality. With these changes probably the international grapes will begin to decrease. Twenty years ago some people wanted to increase the international proportion allowed, but now this is anachronistic; people are increasing Sangiovese and indigenous grapes," Sergio Zingarelli explains. "Planting the vineyards with new clones, at higher density, allows us to make 100% Sangiovese without needing any help from other varieties," says Mario Nunzinate, of Colognole in Chianti Rufina.

Regulations for the various types of wine in Chianti Classico specify the length of time required for aging, but do not specify the type of container. Botti are the traditional oval containers for aging red wines; most often around 60 hl, they are usually made from Slavonian oak, which comes from Croatia and is milder than French oak. Usually botti are used for about 15 years, so there is very little influence from new oak. In the last thirty years, there's been a move to use barriques of French oak, which produce a softer rounder, more "international" wine, although in the past decade there's been some backing off towards tonneaux, which are larger, and have a less obvious effect.

There's still some difference between those who believe that the true typicity of Chianti is best brought out by monovarietal Sangiovese and those who believe in keeping Chianti's long tradition of being a blended wine, but by using better quality varieties for the minor part of the blend. As Paolo de Marchi of Isole e Olena says, the real issue is to make the best wine. "Blending should not be used to improve poor results with Sangiovese, but to bring in a variety with complementary qualities that increases complexity... The pressure to make Chianti just from Sangiovese is taking things to excess."

The New Chianti

The success of the super-Tuscans has partially allowed Chianti to by-pass the arguments about typicity that have occurred in other regions as modern techniques of viticulture and vinification have changed wine styles. It's easier to make a super-Tuscan than to fight for the soul of Chianti. But what should Chianti taste like? The admission of international varieties has diluted the focus on Sangiovese, and many producers believe that the increase to 20% of nontraditional varieties was one step too far. On the other hand, Chianti has always been a blended wine, albeit dominated by Sangiovese, and it's not surprising that the blend should change over time. Whether or not the wine is blended, the slightly acidic, bright red cherry fruits of the past have generally given way to slightly deeper and darker flavors, following the trend of many other wine regions.

The requirements to include low quality black or white grapes, and the limit on the amount of Sangiovese, forced some quality producers out of the DOC; because they wanted to use 100% Sangiovese or to exclude some other varieties, they labeled their wines as IGT Toscana. Recent revisions of the rules have retroactively validated their response. This has all led to a definite improvement in quality, but the genie is out of the bottle, and the best wines (even those which would qualify under the new rules) are usually labeled as IGT Toscana. When you ask Chianti producers whether they would consider relabeling those super-Tuscans that would now qualify as Chianti, they usually shrug and say that they would like to help improve the DOCG, but their wine is now universally recognized as a super-Tuscan.

Trying to get away from the impression that Chianti Classico is always second best, the Consorzio introduced a new classification in 2013, adding Gran Selezione as a new top tier (with effect from the 2010 vintage). Previously wines were divided between Chianti Classico as such and the higher level of Riserva. Now there are three levels. Chianti Classico must age for twelve months, Riserva for 24 months, and Gran Selezione for 30 months. The aging requirements and the other differences in the rules between Riserva and Gran Selezione, are not really significant. Grapes for Gran Selezione must come from an estate's own vineyards, but the wine can be a blend or selection of lots; the restriction just means that it cannot include purchased grapes.

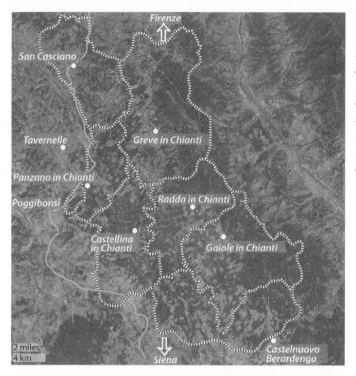

Chianti Classico has several areas, although there are no official sub-zones. Climate and terroir vary considerably.

This was clearly a compromise. Sergio Zingarelli gave a big sigh when I asked why the top wine classification doesn't represent special terroirs. There was something of a desire to make Gran Selezione reflect single vineyards, but pressures in the Consorzio were too strong to allow it. As one example, Ruffino's Ducale Oro is a powerful leading brand, formerly a Riserva, which they wanted to move to Gran Selezione. But it doesn't come from a single vineyard, it is a blend from two estates (actually quite close by). "How do you say no to Ruffino," an informant in the Consorzio explained.

There is in fact something of a move towards producing single vineyard wines from what the producers regard as their grand crus; usually these are described as Vigneto or Vigna followed by the name of the vineyard. There is a trend for these to be Gran Selezione. "Probably 80-90% of Gran Selezione come from single vineyards," says Sergio Zingarelli.

Gran Seleziones must be approved by a committee, which is intended to ensure that they live up to the demands for a top tier, which was not the case with Riserva, and this may very well be the most significant difference. It's a secret how many wines are rejected for the category, but it's claimed that approval is definitely not pro forma.

Reference Wines for Gran Selezione from Single Vineyards

Barone Ricasoli, Castello di Brolio

Castello d'Albola, Il Solatio

Castello Di Ama, San Lorenzo

Castello Di Volpaia, Il Puro

Fattoria Di Fèlsina, Colonia

Fontodi, Vigna del Sorbo

Rocca Delle Macìe, Sergio Zingarelli

The first releases of Gran Selezione were almost all cuvées that previously had been labeled as Riserva. New cuvées are now being created for Gran Selezione, but it's too early to say whether this will dominate or whether Gran Selezione will in effect be a selection of the best wines from the former Riserva category. I was sceptical when I tasted the first releases of Gran Selezione: they were very good, but seemed more like a super-set of the old Riservas than anything really different. Since then, however, there has been a significant improvement in quality and interest of Gran Selezione. The number of Gran Seleziones has increased, with 84 approved in the most recent vintage; the majority still come from the same sources as wines previously labeled as Riservas; some are new cuvées (usually from single vineyards), and a few are wines that previously were labeled as IGT Toscana. About a quarter of Chianti Classico producers now have a Gran Selezione.

One big question is whether Gran Selezione will be competitive with the super Tuscans. "The problem is that the top wine is often not labeled as Chianti Classico," says Sergio Zingarelli. "I planted a new vineyard fifteen years ago to be my top wine, but if there wasn't Gran Selezione it would have been an IGT." It would definitely be a mark of success for Gran Selezione if super-Tuscans were relabeled into the new category. There are mixed opinions about this. "One of the intentions of Gran Selezione was to lure back IGTs to the Chianti Classico, but it hasn't worked very well," says Roberto Stucchi at Badia a Coltibuono. "You can't go back," flatly says Giovanna Stianti at Castello di Volpaia.

Riserva and Gran Selezione tend to have a higher proportion of Sangiovese than Chianti Classico in general, perhaps reflecting the fact that they come from riper grapes, so the inclusion of other varieties is less necessary. Indeed, there's a tendency to use 100% Sangiovese at the level of Gran Selezione.

It's not straightforward to compare Gran Selezione with Riserva directly, because many producers switched the label when the new regulations were approved, but some producers have cuvées in both categories. In these cases, the Gran Selezione is usually just a touch more intense than the Riserva, just as the Riserva is usually a touch more intense than the Chianti Classico, although the difference has narrowed in recent years due to the general improvement in the quality of Chianti Classico.

The wines are altogether richer and deeper, often showing a mix of red and black fruits as opposed to the bright red cherries of old, and perhaps the real message is the improvement of quality all round. Sara Pontemolesi, winemaker at Antinori, made a fair summary of the change in recent years: "We are really defining the style of the wine now, we used to be concerned with the quality, but now we have the quality we can focus on the style of the wine."

The introduction of Gran Selezione was not universally accepted by producers, although some who were against it are now making wines in the category, and it is becoming accepted as the new top tier of Chianti Classico. It's possible that Gran Selezione will finally make the top Chianti Classicos competitive on the international circuit. But one of the criticisms is that this may drive a change in style. "One of the things I don't like about Gran Selezione is that the tasting panel favors more modern international wines. It sends the message that bigger wines are better," says Roberto Stucchi. Reliability will enhance the reputation of Chianti, but some producers still feel that this isn't the main issue. "The idea that grapes should come from your own vineyards makes no sense. The issue shouldn't be the source, it should be the quality of the grapes," says Giovanna Stianti.

Terroirs of Chianti

"The real need here is to clarify Chianti's zones and vineyards, which isn't being done," says Sebastiano Castiglioni of Querciabella, who is staying out of the Gran Selezione system, and focusing on single vineyard wines. Over the various sub-areas of Chianti Classico, there are significant differences in climate (which becomes warmer going from north to south), altitude (with the highest vineyards well up mountains at up to 600m elevation), and of course soil types.

There are eight different communes within Chianti Classico, but although producers may be conscious of their locations, they do not have much impact for the consumer. There's a tendency for wines from the warmer areas to be richer—Castellina in Chianti or Castelnuova Berardenga, for example—but with improvements in viticulture there's also a tendency for Sangiovese to be planted at higher altitudes than used to be thought desirable, which gives a finer quality.

Chianti is pretty hilly, and vineyards are usually between 250m and 500m elevation (with the upper limit 100m or more higher than it used to be before global warming). A mountain range marks the eastern border of Chianti Classico, and protects against cold weather. Most vineyards face south or southwest. The major soil types are galestro (highly friable shale coming from compressed clay), alberese (a calcareous marl resembling limestone), and arenaria (sandstone, known locally as macigno).

All Chianti Classico is local. Producers usually have vineyards only in their own communes, often closely around the winery. You might think this would place some emphasis on identifying different subzones, but even aside from political considerations, one of the difficulties in defining subzones is that the geology does not conform with the communal boundaries; for example, the southern part of Radda in Chianti and the northern part of Gaiole in Chianti are both extremely calcareous, but the southern part of Gaiole in Chianti is completely different.

"Appellation and IGT are the core of the Tuscan problem," says Paolo di Marchi at Isole e Olena. "The wines that have pulled the region up are IGT. Subzones organized by communes (which are basically administrative units) would not make any sense, because they vary so much in size and in the variety of terroirs within each. A classification along Burgundian lines might make sense but would not be politically possible." The issue of subzones is contentious, to say the least, and it seems unlikely they will be introduced at present. "If we divided by soils and geography we would have to have 100 different classifications," says Sergio Zingarelli.

Chianti seems to be evolving towards two extreme styles. I think of them as red fruit and black fruit. What you might call traditional shows lively red fruits with a spectrum in the direction of sour red cherries, with a tang of savory acidity at the end. This tends to dominate the Chianti Classicos *tout court*. The black fruit wines make a more modern impression, with greater density on a softer palate, less obvious acidity, and sometimes tannins evident at the end. There may be a tendency for the modern class to include more in the way of international varieties, and more often to be matured in barriques, but you can find both 100% Sangiovese and blended wines in either category, and wines matured in the traditional large casks in either category. Gran Selezione tend to show more weight (and more alcohol), with some moving in the direction of the smoothness of Brunello.

I would not say it's a mistake to use barriques or new oak, but the effect is to reduce the typicity of Sangiovese from Chianti, that delicious savory counterpoise to the red fruits. For my taste, it's the wines in the traditional, red fruit category that really express the freshness I expect in Chianti, but there are lovely wines in both categories, and it may well be that the more "modern" wines have greater success in today's market.

Reference Wines for Monovarietal Sangiovese
Chianti Classico Gran Selezione
Fattoria Di Fèlsina, Colonia
Fontodi, Vigna del Sorbo
Barone Ricasoli, Colledilà
Castello Di Volpaia, Il Puro
IGT Toscana
Badia A Coltibuono, Sangioveto
Fontodi, Flaccianello della Pieve
Isole E Olena, Cepparello
Montevertine, Le Pergole Torte

With the change in the rules in Chianti Classico, and the introduction of Gran Selezione, the honors for the top monovarietal Sangiovese wines are split between Gran Selezione and super-Tuscans. The best known are still in the super-Tuscan category, but the gap is narrowing.

The development of top quality monovarietal Sangiovese in the Chianti area gives a chance to compare the character of the variety in different areas. Chianti at its best shows the savory side of Sangiovese while Montalcino shows a richer, more chocolaty side. Montepulciano makes a less refined impression, partly due to more clay in the soil. Perhaps greater density of fruits hides minerality in Montalcino, which is tauter, the fruits are more compact, less acid, less overly mineral, and the cherry fruits are more black than sour red. The big challenge for Gran Selezione is to equal the quality of Montalcino, but in the style of Chianti Classico.

Brunello di Montalcino

In Montalcino just to the south, no one was paying much attention to red wine, until led by producer Biondi-Santi, Brunello di Montalcino emerged as one of the best red wines of Italy in the 1970s. Now there is no real challenge to Brunello di Montalcino as home of the greatest Sangiovese wines, except perhaps for one or two super-Tuscans.

Sangiovese is the grape that typifies Tuscany, but Brunello di Montalcino stands alone in its history of making wine from 100% Sangiovese. Before the 1880s, Montalcino was known for sweet wines made from the Moscadello grape (a little Moscadello di Montalcino is still made). When the vineyards were attacked by oïdium, they were replanted with Sangio-

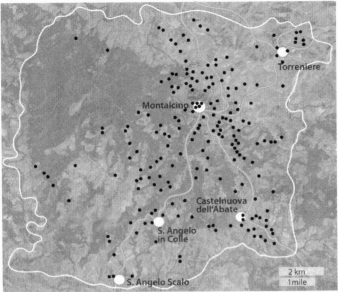

The Montalcino DOCG describes a circle (boundary in white) around the town of Montalcino. Wineries (black circles) extend to the north and south of the town.

vese (more resistant to oïdium and already used in neighboring Chianti and Montepulciano).

Brunello di Montalcino dates from 1890, but through the 1920s there were only four producers bottling wine under its name; even through the 1950s there were fewer than fifteen producers, because most producers were bottling their wines as Chianti Colli Senesi. Brunello di Montalcino was defined as a DOC in 1966—the Consorzio was created in 1967 with 25 members cultivating only 80 ha—but really revived only in the 1970s. In 1980, it was the first region in Italy to become a DOCG. Brunello di Montalcino has now far outstripped Chianti on the international market, being the only traditional wine of Tuscany to vie with the price level of the super-Tuscans.

The production area coincides with the communal territory of Montalcino, 40 km to the south of Siena, more or less a circle with a diameter of 16 km centered on the old town of Montalcino, at an elevation of about 700m. The terroir is varied. The area is divided into two parts: to the north is the original region; plantings in the south are more recent. Regions to the north and east are high in clay and volcanic soils, but to the south and west there is a high proportion of calcareous soils resembling those of Chianti. The climate of the northern half resembles Chianti, milder and wetter

All roads lead to Montalcino. The town occupies a high point that controls all routes through the appellation.

than the southern part, which is warmer and drier. The grapes ripen more slowly in the northern and higher altitude vineyards close to the town of Montalcino, and produce aromatic wines of greater finesse than those from the southern slopes, which tend to be fuller and richer. There is about a two week difference in harvest dates. Roughly one third of the vineyards are in the northern half, with the majority in the south.

Producers often have vineyards in both the south and north; blending between them has traditionally been regarded as the route to getting the greatest complexity, but that has now somewhat given way to the introduction of single vineyard wines. Looking at extremes, the most elegant wines come from around the hill of Montosoli in the north, and the most powerful wines from the area of Sant'Angelo in the southwest. (The largest producers are located at Sant'Angelo, which accordingly accounts for a more than a third of Brunello production.) The rules used to limit plantings for the DOC to below 600 m, because of global warming the limitation has been lifted in the belief that grapes can ripen fully at higher elevations.

The original regulations required long aging in oak (five years for the Riserva), which would admittedly tame the tannins, but often introduced oxidation. Regulations have changed to encourage a more modern style, by bringing the required maturation period in oak down to two years. Riservas spend a year longer before they are released, but the legal difference is only how long the bottle is held before it is released to the market (al-

Located in the northeast, the Montosoli hill is one of the most prestigious sites in Montalcino. Elevation is about 300 m.

though many producers do use Riserva to describe their best wines). Regulations have also reduced the minimum level of acidity, encouraging softer wines more in line with international trends.

The origins of Riservas vary quite a bit. Sometimes they are essentially the same wine aged longer; in the past the wines sometimes did not stand up to the long aging that was required, and the Riservas could seem a bit tired or over-extracted compared to the regular cuvée, but this has ceased to be a problem since the period was reduced to two years. Some Riservas come from barrel selections, but there's an increasing tendency for them to come from old vines or special plots; many Riservas are now single vineyard wines. Some producers make Riservas, or other single vineyard wines, only in the top vintages.

When should you drink Brunello? The dilemma of the modern era is expressed by Stefano Colombini at Fattoria dei Barbi. "Of course, Brunello was made to be drunk old, but now we have to do something difficult, to produce wine that will age but that can be drunk on release, rounder with less aggressive tannins, but capable of long aging. This was technically quite hard, but we did it."

When the wine is ready depends on the vintage; in 2016 the lighter 2011 vintage was more or less ready to drink, but the weightier 2010 vintage required another couple of years. Most Riservas take longer and probably will not be ready until, say, close to a decade after the vintage.

Types of Wine in Montalcino

Rosso di Montalcino	Must age one year, but does not have to be in wood.
Brunello di Montalcino	Must age 2 years in wood, and cannot be released until 5 years old.
Brunello di Montalcino Riserva	Must age 30 months in wood, and cannot be released until 6 years old.

Of course, this depends on your tolerance for tannins: for those accustomed to the more extracted wines of the New World, Brunello's may well seem ready within a couple of years after release.

Modernists and Traditionalists

Brunello di Montalcino is traditionally described as having savory aromas and flavors, with notes of tobacco and leather, but (as elsewhere) changes in winemaking have resulted in more forward, fruitier wines that can be drunk much younger than previously. Style is perhaps now more determined by whether the producer is a traditionalist (maturing the wine in large old casks of Slavonian oak) or a modernist (using small barriques of new French oak). Another view comes from Guido Orzalesi of Altesino, who says that while the type of wood treatment used to be the difference between modernists and traditionalists, now it's more a matter of extraction, with modernists going for greater extraction in the international style, while traditionalists go for a more restrained elegance. (Claudio Basla, Altesino's winemaker, is a bit rueful about his reputation for having introduced barriques into Montalcino; it's true Altesino was the first to use them in the area, but this was not in fact for the Brunello.) Is it an exaggeration to say that the traditional wines are about red fruits, but that the modernist style is all about black fruits?

Maturation in barrique certainly smoothens the wine, adding an overlay of vanillin or other oaky notes that calm down that animal pungency. (Blending in other varieties can have a similar effect, although this is not allowed in Montalcino.) In good years, Brunello has no need of this, with the grapes achieving a ripeness that shows as tobacco, leather, even a note of chocolate on the finish. Personally, I find the traditional style wonderfully distinctive from international-style wines, giving wines of real character; while admitting that the best modernists make wines which retain enough of that character to be modern in style yet identifiable as Brunello, I like to see those intensely savory notes of traditional Sangio-

Biondi Santi	Traditionalist
Barbi	
Salvioni	
Case Basse di Soldera	
Il Poggione	
Camigliano	
La Palazzetta	
Pertimali	
Lisini	
Caprili	
Argiano	
Col d'Orcia	
Ciacci Piccolomini d'Aragona	
Canalicchio di Sopra	
Cerbaiona	
Donatella Colombini	
Sassodisole	
Poggio Antico	
Mastrojanni	
Villa Poggio Salvi	
Casanova di Neri	
San Filippo	
Carpazo	
Castiglion del Bosco	
Pian Delle Vigne	
Valdicava	
Castello Romitorio	
Talenti	
Altesino	
Val di Suga	
Silvio Nardi	
Luce Della Vite	
Banfi	
Gaja	Modernist
Siro Pacenti	

Producers range from those committed to traditional production to modernists, with many in between.

vese. There's enough overt difference in style for producers to characterize themselves as traditionalists or modernists. Of course, it's not always so simple; some producers age for one year in botti and one year in barriques, while others may mature some wines in botti, but use barriques for others. If there is a trend, it's to mature the general Brunello cuvée in botti, but use a proportion of barriques for special cuvées, but there is certainly no fixed rule.

Rosso di Montalcino

In addition to Brunello di Montalcino itself, there is a second DOC called Rosso di Montalcino. This can be used as a second label, so pro-

Reference Wines for Rosso di Montalcino
Altesino
Barbi
Canalicchio di Sopra
Cerbaiona
Ciacci Piccolomini d'Aragona, Rossofonte
Col d'Orcia
Il Poggione
Pian Delle Vigne
Sassodisole
Valdicava
Villa Poggio Salvi
Single Vineyard Rosso di Montalcino
Caparzo, La Caduta
Col d'Orcia, Banditella
Il Poggione, Leopoldo Franceschi
These wines give a good preview of the style of the producer's Brunello.

ducers can declassify wines that don't meet their standard for Brunello itself. Like Brunello, Rosso di Montalcino must be made from 100% Sangiovese, but the aging regime is much shorter, six months in oak and one year in total before release.

The regulations controlling production of Rosso have changed. Originally vineyards were divided into those classified for Brunello (about 2,000 ha) or for Rosso (about 500 ha). Vineyards classified for Brunello could be used to produce either Brunello or Rosso, but vineyards classified as Rosso could be used only to produce Rosso. Assignments were not permanent: a producer could move the classification from one vineyard to another, just as long as the total area of each type stayed the same. Now the system has been replaced by a more direct allocation of a proportion of Brunello versus Rosso for the vineyard total. As before, some Rossos are effectively a separate production, coming from particular plots, whereas others are in effect second wines declassified from Brunello.

There is no general agreement on whether Rosso should be a "baby Brunello" or something different. The range runs from simple entry-level wines to wines that preview the Brunello. "It's a bad attribute of producers to have played with Rosso to make so many things, there've been years of mistakes," says Giacomo Neri at Casanova di Neri. Some producers regard

Located close to the southern boundary of Montalcino, Castello Banfi has one of the largest wine factories in Europe, where wines from surrounding regions as well as Montalcino are made.

Rosso as a wine in its own right, although less complex than Brunello, and lots that aren't good enough for Rosso are declassified become IGT Toscana. Some take Rosso seriously enough to produce single vineyard Rossos.

One common use of the Rosso classification is for young vineyards that have been replanted; when they become older, they are likely to be used for Brunello production. Since total production of Rosso is about three quarters of that of Brunello, a significant amount of wine potentially allowed to make Brunello must in fact be declassified to Rosso. The vintages of 2002 and 2014 were extreme cases in which some producers declassified their whole crop to Rosso (the result being that some Rossos, such as Valdicava or Canalicchio di Sopra, which are always at the top anyway, really show increased quality and character).

The Battle for Sangiovese

One factor in modernizing the region was the arrival of Villa Banfi in 1978. The owners are the American Mariani brothers, whose fortune came from selling Lambrusco (sweet, red, and fizzy) in the American market in the 1970s. They purchased large tracts of land, terraformed the landscape, including the construction of six lakes to provide water for irrigation, established a huge modern facility, and started to produce a wide range of wines of all types, from dry to sweet, white to red, and still to sparkling to fortified. With 155 hectares of Brunello, they are the largest producer in Montalcino, but this is dwarfed by their production of more commercial wines from a wide variety of grapes and locations.

Banfi remain controversial: there is acknowledgment that they helped to develop the American market for Brunello, but concern that they changed the landscape to benefit varieties other than Sangiovese. Some see the move towards a more international style as a consequence: "Banfi opened the door to the US market, then the whole Montalcino region started to use the smaller barrels for this reason," one producer says.

Does 100% Sangiovese necessarily make the best wine? It's sometimes felt to be a little hard, and there've always been rumors of blending with other grapes to soften it. These came to a head in the Brunellopoli scandal of 2008 when the Italian news magazine, L'Espresso, reported that 20 producers were being investigated for fraud under suspicion that they had blended Brunello with other varieties (typically Cabernet Sauvignon to bump up the color and structure). The investigation was supposedly sparked by a well-known producer who was indignant at others' continued flouting of the rules.

Million of bottles were seized by the investigating magistrate to be tested to see whether they included other varieties. After two years, the investigation somewhat fizzled out, with an inconclusive report, and the declassification of some of the seized wines to IGT. Some producers were fined, but the names have never been released. The Consorzio (producers' association) considered the matter, and decided by an overwhelming vote that Brunello should remain 100% Sangiovese. Many producers say that allowing other varieties would diffuse Brunello's identity in the way they believe happened in Chianti when international varieties were admitted.

Superficially the argument has been resolved, but a troubling issue underlies it. Production of Brunello di Montalcino has more or less doubled in a decade. This means that it has almost certainly been extended beyond the sites that are optimum for growing Sangiovese, creating pressure to include other varieties to "help" the Sangiovese. As Antonio Galloni remarks in The Wine Advocate, "Brunello is a wine whose fame is based on the supposedly special qualities of the Sangiovese Grosso clone... Allowing for the use of other grapes is a (not so) tacit admission that perhaps Sangiovese from Montalcino was never all that special in the first place and/or that the grape has been planted in an exorbitant number of places to which it is fundamentally ill-suited." The only way out of the box is to pull back Brunello to the best sites, and to use some other label for wine from other sites (with or without other varieties in the blend).

In addition to Brunello and Rosso di Montalcino, there are two other DOCs in the Montalcino area. Moscadello di Montalcino is a (usually cheap) sparkling wine from Muscat, which is not much more than a remnant of history at this point. Only fifteen estates make Moscadello, and styles vary from sweet (because fermentation is blocked) to late harvest or sparkling.

Sant'Animo was introduced as a catch-all DOC to allow producers to make wines from other varieties, but it has really failed to make any impact. Those producers in Montalcino who make wines from other varieties usually label them as IGT Toscana, and describe them as super-Tuscans.

Not all producers in Montalcino are necessarily committed to the appellation, at least in the sense that it is their main focus. Although this is the most prestigious appellation in Tuscany, and one of the most prestigious in Italy (second to Barolo), the lure of the super-Tuscans is hard to resist. Smaller producers may make only Brunello and Rosso, but larger producers often have a super-Tuscan, made from varieties other than Sangiovese, at a price level comparable to their Brunello.

Bolgheri: Challenge to Bordeaux?

The land used to be marshy but has been drained. (At one time it was famous for its population of malarial mosquitoes.) The soil is stony. The climate is maritime. Dominant varieties are Cabernet Sauvignon, Cabernet Franc, and Merlot. The major producers have large estates; often enough it is fairly difficult to arrange visits. Sounds like Bordeaux? No, it's the new area of Bolgheri on the Tuscan coast, where thirty years ago there were virtually no vineyards, but which today produces some of Italy's most famous wines from Bordeaux blends. It is an exaggeration to say that the explosive growth of Bolgheri was due to familial rivalry between the original owners of the Sassicaia and Ornellaia estates, but certainly these two great houses had a great deal to do with the success of the region. (All those wines with "aia" at the end of the name, by the way, identify Tuscan origins, because "aia" is Tuscan dialect meaning "the place of.")

The story of Sassicaia, the original super-Tuscan, perfectly illustrates the contortions of the Italian DOC system. The Marquis Incisa della Rocchetta, from an old Tuscan family, acquired the Tenuta San Guido estate in the 1930s by marriage. Inspired by a love of Bordeaux, in 1944 he planted a hectare each of Cabernet Sauvignon and Cabernet Franc at the estate; and in 1965 extended the plantings to new vineyards of Cabernet Sauvignon and Cabernet Franc. Initially the wine was consumed only in the family; the first vintage of Sassicaia to be offered on the open market was the 1968.

There was no precedent in the modern Italian system for producing Cabernet Sauvignon in Tuscany, so the wine was sold only as Vino da Tavola. (However, there is nothing new under the Tuscan sun; a century earlier, a survey of foreign grapes growing in Italy said, "Even the best Tus-

Ornellaia nestles into the hillside in an estate including 50 ha of vineyards.

can wines improve notably if Cabernet is added in small quantities. Especially worthy of note are the results obtained by blending Cabernet with Sangiovese.")

Although the Marquis was somewhat uncertain about its potential longevity when the wine was launched, Sassicaia rapidly achieved legendary status as a rival to the top wines of Bordeaux. The 1985 is generally reckoned to have been one of the best wines produced in Italy. Sassicaia sparked the whole super-Tuscan phenomenon of exceptional wines that did not fit any DOC, either because they came from outside DOC areas or because they used a blend of grape varieties not permitted in the DOCs. Eventually it became untenable for one of Italy's top wines to be merely a Vino da Tavola, and a special DOC was created in 1994, Bolgheri Sassicaia, just for the one wine.

Not to be outdone in the family, Marquis Lodovico Antinori, a cousin of Sassicaia's Nicolò Incisa, created Tenuta Dell'Ornellaia in 1981 with vineyards adjacent to those of Sassicaia. Perhaps partly driven by a wish to be distinct from Sassicaia, the vineyards were planted with Cabernet Sauvignon and Merlot. The first vintage was harvested in 1985, and the winery was constructed in 1987. Among the vineyards are the 7 ha Masseto hill, where the clay is several meters deep, and the Merlot gave such extraordinary results that it was diverted to a separate wine. (The hill is not actually that high, only about 120m.)

Ornellaia itself actually did not contain much Merlot until the subsequent purchase and planting of the Bellaria vineyard a little to the north of Bolgheri. More recently, the Merlot has been decreasing to make room for a little Cabernet Franc. But the ownership has undergone a complete change. The Mondavi winery of California took a minority interest in the estate in 1999, then went into partnership with the Frescobaldi family; and

Types of Wine in Bolgheri	
Bolgheri (red)	May contain up to 100% Cabernet Sauvignon, Merlot, or Sangiovese.
Bolgheri (white)	Can be Vermentino or blends of Sauvignon Blanc or Trebbiano.
Bolgheri Superiore	Minimum alcohol 12.5%, must age one year in wood, cannot be released until 2 years old.

then Frescobaldi purchased the estate outright after Constellation Brands took over Mondavi.

Following the lead of Sassicaia and Ornellaia, Bolgheri remains devoted to Bordeaux varieties, with blends resembling the Médoc; in addition there is a small amount of Syrah and an even smaller amount of Sangiovese. "Bolgheri is not a suitable area for Sangiovese, it does not do well here," says Sebastiano Rosso, the winemaker at Sassicaia. Perhaps that is why Bolgheri's fame had to wait until the Bordeaux varieties were tried. How far have producers in Bolgheri followed Sassicaia's example? "I think they are doing something different, because when they came out the style of wine was being influenced by the New World and everyone started to look for a lot of extraction and alcohol," comments Marquis Nicolò Incisa.

When the IGT Toscana classification was created, Bolgheri provided its best wines, colloquially described as super-Tuscans, but a general Bolgheri DOC was created in 1994. It allows a smorgasbord of varieties rather than attempting to impose any uniform style. The original rules required red wines to have at least 10%, and up to a maximum of 80% Cabernet Sauvignon, 70% Merlot, or 70% Sangiovese. Now a change in rules allows 100% of Cabernet Sauvignon, Cabernet Franc, or Merlot. Bolgheri's wines are among Italy's top wines, yet Bolgheri is only a humble DOC; perhaps in due course it will be deemed worthy to join Chianti and others in the DOCG category.

There are two general classifications in Bolgheri: Bolgheri and Bolgheri Superiore. There's a tendency to use Bolgheri for the entry-level wines and Superiore for the wines that started out as super-Tuscans, but the name of the producer is far more important, and the classification is useful more to distinguish the wines within a producer's range than to provide any indication of grape varieties or aging processes.

Some of the original super-Tuscans are now found under the umbrella of the Bolgheri DOC. Some remain in the IGT Toscana classification, such as Masseto, originally excluded because it is 100% Merlot. Wines that

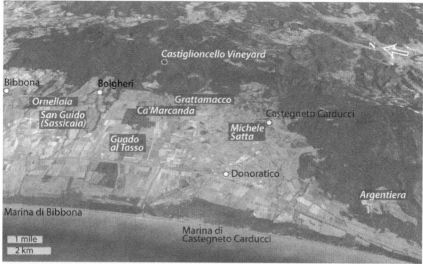

The vineyards of Bolgheri lie in a narrow band between the sea and the mountains. The DOC includes 1,100 ha of vineyards belonging to 40 producers.

started as IGT Toscana and later converted to Bolgheri DOC are still usually regarded as super-Tuscans. Generally Bolgheri Superiore is used for those at the top end that might be regarded as super-Tuscans, and Bolgheri Rosso is used for second labels or lesser wines. But some producers still say that super-Tuscan is the description that has recognition in the marketplace. Winemaker Axel Heinz at Ornellaia thinks that "wine produced for cash flow should be labeled IGT Toscana, but Bolgheri should stand for something more ambitious."

Does Bolgheri have a distinct identity? "In the last twenty years Bolgheri has developed its identity and style," says winemaker Marco Ferrarese at Guado al Tasso. "The blend is similar (to super-Tuscans in the Chianti area). The style is quite different. The wine is warmer with the character more oriented towards red fruit, the acidity is lower, the tannins are sweet and rich. So the wine is ready to drink at two years, but with good longevity. Our ambition is to make wine you can compare with Bordeaux, but we have our identity. It can be difficult to tell whether you have Cabernet or Merlot sometimes. So whatever gives the identity it's not the variety." Fabio Motto at Michele Satta has a similar view: "We feel it in the grapes, we have softness in the tannins, there is always roundness in the mouth, this is the style of Bolgheri."

"Bolgheri is a wine of the south," says Axel Heinz. "It's a Mediterranean version of the Bordeaux climate. Bolgheri has a special combination of opulence, ripeness, and freshness, there's an almost exotic ripeness in the nose, but not explosive like young California Cabernet Sauvignon, there is a spiciness, a mintiness, and in the mouth there's sweetness, but compared to the other southern wines they always finish dry and fresh, that's the special feature of this place."

Although the blend in Bolgheri resembles Bordeaux's left bank—typically about two thirds Cabernet Sauvignon, with Merlot as the second variety, and a small amount of Cabernet Franc—the characteristic softness of the palate more resembles Bordeaux's right bank. It might be fair to say that insofar as Bolgheri resembles Bordeaux (and I'm not sure there is that much resemblance), its character lies somewhere between the left and right banks: there is always structure (at least when the wines are based on Cabernet) but there is also that telltale softness or lushness. Perhaps the single word most appropriate to describe the various wines of Bolgheri is *juicy:* there is a rich impression of overt fruits, but remaining distinctly Old World.

Super-Tuscans

The origins of the super-Tuscan phenomenon go back to the inflexibility of the DOC system, in particular its exclusion of nonindigenous grape varieties, which led to a revolution when some top wines were classified under a generic Vino da Tavola label. Propelled by the incongruity of Sassicaia and other wines achieving great reputation while in the lowly category of vino da Tavolo, the new category of IGT Toscana was created in 1992 for wines that did not conform to DOC(G) regulations but that rose above table wine, but this took off in an unexpected way when the top wines in this category became known as super-Tuscans.

Super-Tuscans aren't easy to define. Axel Heinz points out that Tuscany is a large area, and is amused by the occasional requests for a vintage chart for super-Tuscans. But let's suppose for a moment that there was actually an equivalent for a DOC for the super-Tuscan. What would its regulations be? It would have to allow any proportion of any of the grapes of Cabernet Sauvignon, Cabernet Franc, Merlot, Syrah, or Sangiovese. Perhaps the rule would state that a super-Tuscan could be any red variety or combination of varieties so long as it was aged in barrique for any period of time. It could come from any wine-producing region in Tuscany, so what would the vintage chart say—would it reflect conditions in the mountains of Chianti or at the seaside of Maremma? Perhaps the most sensible unifying regulation in order to stop the riff-raff from making wines labeled IGT Toscana would be to specify that there must be a high minimum price!

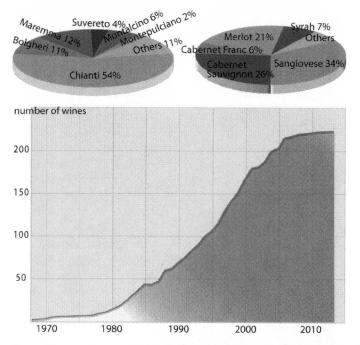

Super Tuscans grew exponentially in the 1990s and leveled off in the 2000s. The pie chart shows the sources of today's super-Tuscans and the overall proportions of grape varieties.

The diffusely defined nature of super-Tuscans makes it difficult to know how much super-Tuscan wine is really produced. Some "super-Tuscans" are produced in tiny amounts, others at more than 100,000 bottles per year. Of Tuscany's annual total production of 40 million cases, about one third is DOC (of which Chianti represents almost two thirds). Probably the entire production of super-Tuscans is below 250,000 cases annually, about half of the production of Brunello di Montalcino.

But somewhat like garage wines in Bordeaux, the effect of the super-Tuscans has been disproportionate. They have raised the bar for the quality of all production in the region, although it must be admitted that their success has made it all but impossible for some DOCs to compete. This is especially evident in Chianti Classico. Super-Tuscans really start where Chianti Classico stops, and it's striking how many Chianti producers now have an IGT Toscana as their most expensive wine.

It's become a moot point what you classify as a super-Tuscan now that many wines that were formerly IGT Toscana are DOC Bolgheri or Maremma. At one point a super-Tuscan was regarded as more or less equivalent to a Bordeaux blend, with a few monovarietals or Syrah-based wines included. Bolgheri and Maremma are still very much focused on international varieties, and Bordeaux varieties now account for about half of the IGT Toscana category, ranging from wines based on Cabernet Sauvignon to 100% Merlots. Overall, today more than a third of IGT Toscana are monovarietal wines.

There's also quite a bit of Syrah; sometimes it is included in a blend (usually with Bordeaux varieties, but there are also some 100% Syrah wines). Syrah in Tuscany gives interesting results, brighter and fresher than the wines of southern France, for example, and can be appealing. Merlot, on the other hand, does not do so well in hot climates, and although it's popular to soften a blend, as a monovarietal it tends generally to give somewhat monotonic flavors that don't reflect the terroir; "Merlot is an unfit grape for Tuscany," flatly says enologist Lorenzo Land.

After starting in Bolgheri, the super-Tuscan phenomenon widened to take in other areas. Chianti has become the most common origin for super-Tuscans, following the lead of Tignanello, a Sangiovese-dominated blend with Cabernet Sauvignon. Tignanello is produced on an estate in the Chianti region, but was labeled as a table wine in 1971, and later became part of the new IGT classification. It contained too much Sangiovese, as well as a small proportion of the Cabernets, to be a Chianti originally, but ironically under the new regulations it could now be a Chianti Classico.

Other wines that would have brought prestige to Chianti are Montevertine's Le Pergole Torte, Fontodi's Flaccianello, or Isole e Olena's Cepparello, all 100% Sangiovese, made from vineyards in the heart of Chianti Classico—but labeled as IGTs originally because monovarietal Sangiovese was not allowed in Chianti at the time, and now perhaps because there's more prestige in being IGT Toscana than Chianti Classico!

This demonstration of the potential of Sangiovese might never have occurred without the spur of the super-Tuscans. Indeed, Sangiovese has now become the best represented single grape in super-Tuscans. A handful of super-Tuscans come from Montalcino, but are not made from Sangiovese, which fetches such high prices under the Brunello di Montalcino label that there is no need to declassify to IGT!

Among Cabernet-based super-Tuscans, there's a difference in the blend from Bolgheri and Chianti. The "average" super-Tuscan in Bolgheri has a distinctly left bank blend: about two thirds Cabernet Sauvignon, with Merlot as the second variety, and a small amount of Cabernet Franc. A Cabernet-dominated super-Tuscan from Chianti is likely to have Sangiovese as the second variety, and sometimes some Merlot. How does a super Tuscan from Chianti differ from one from Bolgheri? "The Cabernet in Solaia [made at the Tignanello estate in Chianti Classico] is more linear, stronger, like stainless steel. Cabernets from Bolgheri are more rounded, more generous," explains Marco Ferrarese.

The super-Tuscans first came to prominence in the 1980s. Some nay-sayers think the movement has run its course, and that people are now tired of powerful international-style wines, but if so, the news has yet to reach Tuscany. In fact, the number of super-Tuscans continues to increase. Including wines produced in the regions of Bolgheri, Chianti, and Montal-cino, there are now well over a hundred super-Tuscans. More than half come from the Chianti region, and of those about half actually could now be classified as Chianti according to current regulations. The most rapidly growing new area is Maremma, just south of Bolgheri. Of course, it's a fine line as to what is a super-Tuscan and what is merely a wine using the IGT Toscana label in the way that was originally intended.

The success of super-Tuscans has led to occasional imitations else-where, but for the most part the "super" concept remains confined to Tuscany. The other region of great repute, Piedmont, has not taken up in-ternational varieties to any great degree. Perhaps the major importance of super-Tuscans is that they gave a great boost to the confidence of produc-ers in Tuscany that they could produce world-class wines.

Vintages

Recent vintages are exercises in extremes. Generally in Tuscany, 2017 has the same problem as everywhere in Europe, with yields greatly re-duced, but high quality. "2017 was a very good vintage for me as an oenologist, the fruit quality is very good, but it is not so good for the owner because quantity is only 30-40%," says Sergio Cantini at Camigliano in Montalcino. Quantity was also reduced in 2016, which was generally a warm year, but not as structured as 2015, which was also warm and pro-duced opulent wines. "If you made bad wine in 2015, it would not be worth going on. It's the best year we've ever had," says Giovanna Stianti at Castello di Volpaia. 2014 was more or less a disaster, 2013 is no more than average, 2012 is an excellent vintage, and depending on location, 2011 or 2010 may be the great year for aging, with the other giving lighter wines for immediate consumption.

Given the variety of grapes and variations in climate, there is no single vintage chart for Tuscany, even though conditions across the region may seem reasonably consistent in any year. Roughly speaking, vintage charts for Bolgheri are likely to represent the success of Cabernet Sauvignon, whereas for Montalcino and Chianti Classico they depend on Sangiovese. Both Sangiovese and Cabernet Sauvignon are late-ripening varieties, but Cabernet is even later, and the gap can make all the difference. "In 1997,

34

Solaia was a great vintage but Tignanello has dusty tannins because of problems in getting to ripeness," says winemaker Renzo Cotarello, describing the Cabernet Sauvignon and Sangiovese-based wines from adjacent vineyards. so super-Tuscans in the Chianti area may not necessarily follow the same rules as Chianti Classico. Even between Chianti Classico and Montalcino, both dependent on Sangiovese, there can be differences; in recent vintages 2010 was the great year in Montalcino, but 2011 was the great year in Chianti Classico.

Vintages in Chianti Classico

Year	Rating	Description
2017		Reduced yields but potentially high quality, although summer was extremely hot.
2016	***	Excellent vintage for Chianti, with rich wines. "I have never seen a vintage like this," says Renzo Cotarella of Antinori.
2015	***	Sunny, hot summer—one of the hottest vintages to date—gave well-structured, rich wines. Some producers called it the vintage of the century.
2014	*	Cool, wet summer saved by September; wines range from elegant to green.
2013	*	A tight vintage, ranging from elegant to lean.
2012	**	Well structured wines generally giving a firm impression.
2011	***	A good start to the decade, ripe and rich.
2010	**	Relatively fresh vintage, early drinking.
2009	*	Rain at start and end of season gave lighter wines.
2008		Average vintage, weakened by rain during season.
2007	***	Best vintage of the decade, aromatic and ripe.
2006	**	Intense wines but over-shadowed by 2007.
2005		Rain during harvest gave lighter wines.
2004	**	A very good vintage, but not as outstanding as in Montalcino.

Vintages in Montalcino

2017		Hot, early vintage, with much reduced yields may give concentrated wines.
2016	***	Promises to be an excellent vintage with concentrated wines.
2015	***	Sunny, hot vintage caused producers to draw parallels with the highly structured 2010 vintage, but 2015 will be ready (relatively) earlier.
2014		A poor vintage to point at which a large proportion of Brunello was declassified to Rosso.
2013	*	Tricky summer with wet start and uneven temperatures followed by Indian summer gave well-structured wines on lighter side, tending to elegance, for drinking 5-10 years after vintage.
2012	**	Good vintage but unusually small, with wines that are ready to drink. Very attractive now.
2011	**	Warm year, wines evolving rapidly and good for drinking in short to mid term.
2010	***	This is a great year, with intense, structured wines, but they will not be ready for a few years.
2009	*	Warm summer gave an early drinking vintage.
2008		Cool, wet conditions, but some elegant wines.
2007		Hot, forward vintage.
2006	**	Powerful, well structured wines that need aging.
2005		Rain during harvest spoiled the vintage, but some nice wines for early drinking.
2004	***	A top vintage, stylish and elegant, widely regarded as a classic.

		Vintages in Bolgheri
2016	**	Hot, dry summer until mid-August, then cooler, leading to comparisons with the well-structured 2008 and 2006 vintages.
2015	***	A very good vintage, as everywhere in Tuscany
2014		Wet conditions gave lighter wines.
2013		Cool rainy start followed by hot dry summer, but good September brought late harvest. Average overall.
2012	*	Hot and dry conditions gave early harvest with intense wines, but not as well balanced as 2011.
2011	**	Dry but not especially hot, very fine wines. A good start to the decade.
2010	*	Inconsistent year due to weather variations in September, but elegant at its best.
2009	*	One of the extremes, hot and dry in July and August, but rain in September; more forceful in style.
2008		Very wet at start, followed by hot, dry conditions; wines are concentrated with higher acidity than usual.
2007	**	Warm at start, then cool in August, but perfect September gave firm fruit expression and more tannic wines.
2006	**	Late, dry vintage gave rich wines and is well regarded.
2005	**	Good conditions in growing season gave wines in fruity style but not as good as 2004.
2004	***	One of the top vintages, ripe but not over-ripe, elegant in style.

Visiting the Region

Bolgheri is quite compact, and all the wineries are within easy reach, many of them off the main road parallel to the coast. It is easy to visit several in a day from a base in Bolgheri itself or Castegneto Carducci. A new tourist attraction (as of 2017) is MUSEM, a wine museum located in an old farm near Castegneto Carducci. Going farther south, it's an hour or so's easy drive to Suvereto or wineries elsewhere in Maremma.

Montalcino is a small area but governed by the principle that all road go to Montalcino. So it takes much longer than you expect to go between wineries in the south and the north, as you have to follow the steep roads up to the town of Montalcino and down again. In planning visits, it is best to group visits by quadrants. Even then, it can take longer than expected from the map to go between wineries, as many roads are unpaved and unmarked. Maps do not distinguish paved and unpaved roads. The locals claim that it is now impossible to pave them as a result of UNESCO's declaration of Montalcino as a World Heritage Site.

Chianti Classico is a large area, more or less extending from Florence to Siena, with villages connected by narrow, winding roads that often go up one side of a valley and then down on the other side. It would be ambitious to try to visit the whole region from a single base, and the best schedule is to organize visits to the southern half separately from the northern half. Possible bases for visits are Castelnuova Berardenga at the southern edge, Gaiole or Radda in Chianti in the center, and Tavernelle or Panzano in Chianti for the north. There's an increasing trend for wineries to have accommodation and restaurants.

Some important producers of Chianti Classico occupy medieval castles or monasteries, reflecting a history in which they were the centers of large farming estates, so a visit combines a tour of the winery with a tour of the historic monument. Baron Ricasoli occupies Castello di Brolio, an imposing fortress with extensive grounds, Castello Vicchiomaggio, Castello d'Albola, and Badia a Coltibuono are all historic sites, and Castello di Volpaia occupies an entire fortified medieval village on a hilltop. All are worth seeing even apart from wine tasting.

Most producers in Chianti sell wine directly to visitors. The same is true in Montalcino and Bolgheri except for a few producers whose wines are in high demand or on allocation, where you can taste but probably will not be able to buy the top cuvées.

An increased focus on oenotourism has made cellar door sales more important to the point where many producers may be disappointed if you do not make a purchase after tasting.

The etiquette of tasting assumes you will spit. A producer will be surprised if you drink the wine. Usually a tasting room or cellar is equipped with spittoons, but ask if you do not see one.

Profiles of Leading Estates

Ratings

★★★	Excellent producers defining the very best of the appellation
★★	Top producers whose wines typify the appellation
★	Very good producers making wines of character that rarely disappoint

Symbols

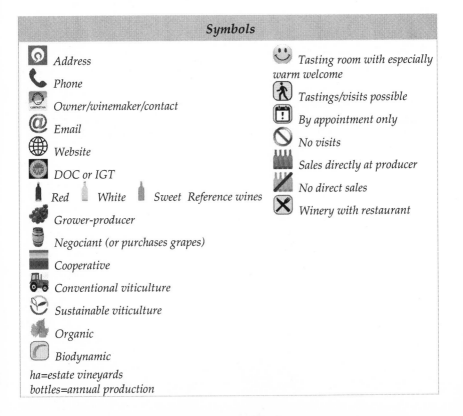

Address

Phone

Owner/winemaker/contact

Email

Website

DOC or IGT

Red   White   Sweet Reference wines

Grower-producer

Negociant (or purchases grapes)

Cooperative

Conventional viticulture

Sustainable viticulture

Organic

Biodynamic

ha=estate vineyards
bottles=annual production

Tasting room with especially warm welcome

Tastings/visits possible

By appointment only

No visits

Sales directly at producer

No direct sales

Winery with restaurant

IGT Toscana

Bibi Graetz   ★★★

TESTAMATTA
TOSCANA

📍 *Via di Vincigliata 19, 50014 Fiesole (FI)*

📞 *(39) 0555 97222*

Bibi Graetz

@ *info@bibigraetz.com*

🌐 *www.bibigraetz.com*

◉ *IGT Toscana*

IGT Toscana, Testamatta

IGT Toscana, Bugia

🍇 *50 ha; 500,000 bottles*

[map p. 42]

Bibi Graetz has a penchant for making wine in unusual places—high up in the hills of Fiesole, overlooking Florence, and on Giglio, a steep and rocky island off the coast of Maremma. Well outside the famous areas, the winery in Fiesole is there because "I was born here. My grandfather bought the house and land, did some farming and made some wine that was sold in bulk. My father planted a 2 ha vineyard here in the 1960s."

Bibi started making wine in 2000, and sources grapes from vineyards all over the area, "like a stripe running through the whole area of Chianti," Bibi says. The approach is the antithesis of the increasing worldwide focus on single vineyards; the wines are blends from multiple sources. "I was in love with old vineyards, so it didn't make any sense to buy land and plant, so I looked for old vineyards. I have long term contracts; we manage vineyards but don't own land. So it doesn't make sense for us to make a single vineyard wine. Our idea is more like a super-Tuscan than a Burgundy concept."

The two major reds, Testamatta and Colore, are labeled as IGT Toscana. Testamatta comes from seven plots and is 100% Sangiovese. Its vivid label reflects the family background in art: Bibi's father is an artist, and so was Bibi before he turned to winemaking. Colore is a selection of the best lots, from the oldest vineyards, and is about a third each of Canaiolo, Colorino, and Sangiovese. The vineyard plots used for Testamatta are usually the same each year; there is a little variation in the Sangiovese used for Colore as it always has the best barrels. "Colore has a little new oak, we look for the lots with more structure, so it has a bit more volume." Tasting barrel samples from the individual vineyards, it becomes clear that Bibi is in love not only with old vineyards, but also with high altitude vineyards; all except one are above 300m. They vary from the cool climate impressions of a plot at high elevation above Greve in Chianti, to the more powerfully structured expression of a south-facing vineyard south of Siena. Variations in oak also contribute, although there is no new oak in Testamatta. In the early years, the wines went into 100% new oak, under the advice of an oenologist, but this changed after 2005. "I don't work with an oenologist any more because I like to do my thing." Today Bibi's view is that, "for Testamatta it is important not to use new oak, we wouldn't have the fruit coming forward. The uniqueness of Testamatta is that we don't impose a style, you don't have the oak, you just have the impression of the grapes coming out." Indeed there is wide vintage variation: 2016 will be a powerful vintage, but 2015 is infinitely elegant.

The white wines all come from Giglio. "It's basically a rock in the middle of the sea, it's a pretty arid climate—it never rains!" Bibi says. "Vineyards go from sea level to 300m. We are planting one at 550m. You can do a big white wine in Giglio, it's not so easy to find a big white from Tuscany." Bibi's whites have their own character. Aside from the entry-level wine, Scopeta, the whites are all 100% Ansonica. Chiozzolo is an orange wine, fermented on skins for 7 days and aged in new oak. Bugia is more conventional, with 90% aged in stainless steel and 10% in wood. In 2016, Bibi produced a white Testamatta for the first time, just 700 bottles. "For Testamatta I took the best parcels, there's no skin contact but it's fermented and aged in 100% new oak. Here I think you go towards a big white wine." The common feature, whether coming from the grapes or from skin contact or oak maturation, is a sense of extract and texture to the palate, almost a sense of austerity to restrain the fruits. These are definitely wines with personality.

Making wine in three places, Bibi is a busy fellow. In addition to the reds of Fiesole and the whites of Giglio, there are entry level wines, part of a negociant activity under the Casamatta name, made in rented space at a larger winery. "Our winery is not big enough to do entry level wine," Bibi explains. It has been difficult to visit the winery, because it's basically a small group of buildings extending from the family house. But this may change as Bibi is thinking about moving into larger space, which would relieve the cramped conditions at the winery, and allow there to be a tasting room. It's not just wine that ferments here: there is a constant whirl of ideas. In the air at the moment are the possibilities of introducing a single vineyard wine or a second wine to Testamatta. This must surely be one of the liveliest wineries in Tuscany.

Chianti Classico

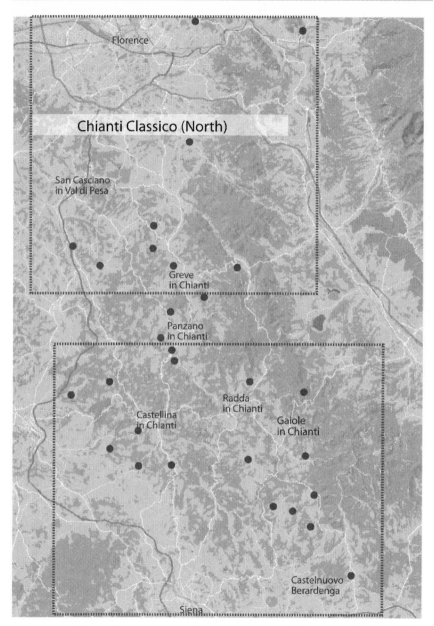

Chianti Classico (North)

Florence

San Casciano
in Val di Pesa

Greve
in Chianti

Panzano
in Chianti

Castellina
in Chianti

Radda
in Chianti

Gaiole
in Chianti

Castelnuovo
Berardenga

Siena

42

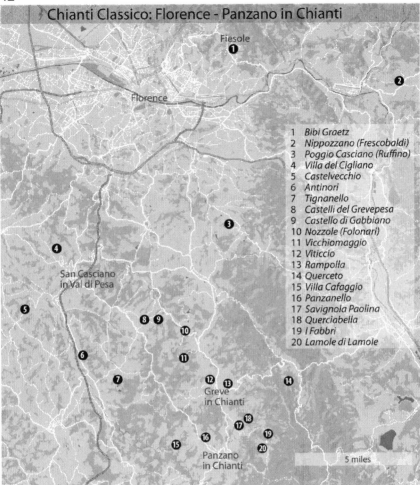

Chianti Classico: Florence - Panzano in Chianti

Fiesole ❶

Florence

❷

1 Bibi Graetz
2 Nippozzano (Frescobaldi)
3 Poggio Casciano (Ruffino)
4 Villa del Cigliano
5 Castelvecchio
6 Antinori
7 Tignanello
8 Castelli del Grevepesa
9 Castello di Gabbiano
10 Nozzole (Folonari)
11 Vicchiomaggio
12 Viticcio
13 Rampolla
14 Querceto
15 Villa Cafaggio
16 Panzanello
17 Savignola Paolina
18 Querciabella
19 I Fabbri
20 Lamole di Lamole

❸

❹

San Casciano
in Val di Pesa

❺

❽ ❾

❻ ❿

❼ ⑪

⑫ ⑬   ⑭
Greve
in Chianti

⑱
⑰

⑮ ⑯   ⑲
⑳
Panzano
in Chianti

5 miles

Chianti Classico: Panzano in Chianti - Castelnuova Berardenga

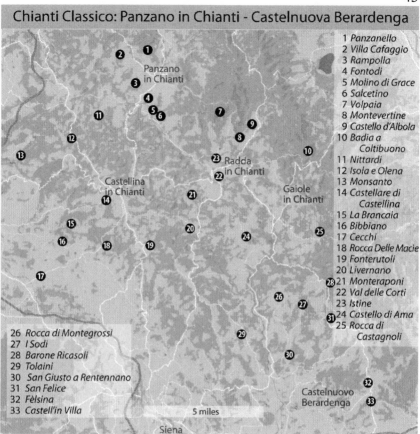

1 Panzanello
2 Villa Cafaggio
3 Rampolla
4 Fontodi
5 Molino di Grace
6 Salcetino
7 Volpaia
8 Montevertine
9 Castello d'Albola
10 Badia a
   Coltibuono
11 Nittardi
12 Isola e Olena
13 Monsanto
14 Castellare di
   Castellina
15 La Brancaia
16 Bibbiano
17 Cecchi
18 Rocca Delle Macie
19 Fonterutoli
20 Livernano
21 Monteraponi
22 Val delle Corti
23 Istine
24 Castello di Ama
25 Rocca di
   Castagnoli

26 Rocca di Montegrossi
27 I Sodi
28 Barone Ricasoli
29 Tolaini
30 San Giusto a Rentennano
31 San Felice
32 Fèlsina
33 Castell'in Villa

Panzano
in Chianti

Radda
in Chianti

Castellina
in Chianti

Gaiole
in Chianti

Castelnuovo
Berardenga

5 miles

Siena

Castello d'Albola ⃰

CASTELLO D'ALBOLA

CHIANTI CLASSICO

CASTELLO D'ALBOLA

⊙ *Via Pian d'Albola 31, 53017 Radda In Chianti*

☎ *(39) 05777 38019*

✉ *Veronique Peeters*

@ *info@albola.it*

🌐 *www.albola.it*

🔘 *Chianti Classico*

🍾 *Chianti Classico, Il Solatio*

🍶 *Chianti Classico Vin Santo*

😊 🏭

🍇 🍂 *140 ha; 800,000 bottles*

[map p. 43]

The Zonin family comes from Veneto and has been in wine since 1821. They own a variety of estates in Italy, including Tuscany, Lombardy, Alto Adige, Puglia, and Sicily, as well as one in Virginia, USA. They purchased Castello d'Albola in 1979. As a property of the Church, the estate dates from 1010, and the castle was built to fortify the hilltop in the battle between Firenze and Siena around 1100. The original stone structure was extended into other buildings during the Renaissance.

Castello d'Albola has some of the highest vineyards in Tuscany, extending from 300m to 700m, with exposures veering from southwest to southeast. "The size of the estate allows us to produce different expressions of Sangiovese," says Matteo Zonin. "Our style is to focus on the expression of Radda in Chianti. Because of our location, alcohol levels reach only 13 or 13.5%. The wines are not so heavy or alcoholic, that's not our style. In 2013 we switched to 100% Sangiovese for all our wines to keep freshness and character of the grapes. We age our wines much longer than the regulations. We like to sell the wine when it is ready."

Chianti Classico spends 1 year in botti and is released at 2.5 years; Riserva spends 1.5 years in wood, 70% in botti and 30% in 2- and 3-year barriques, and is released at 4 years. It is based on a selection of grapes from the best vineyards. Two Gran Selezione are single vineyard wines. The first is a selection of the best lots from half of a 4 ha plot. The Cru, Il Solatio, is higher up and farther south. It is only 1 ha—"in the middle of nowhere"—one of the highest vineyards in Tuscany at 600m. Both Gran

Selezione are produced only in top vintages. The IGT Toscana Acciaiola comes from a plot of old vines near Radda at 400 m. There's a progression of style along the range. The Chianti Classico is always fresh, even in warm vintages, with moderate alcohol, and showing the bite of Sangiovese. The Riserva has greater depth and smoothness, and moves more in a black fruit selection. Gran Selezione Il Solatio is rounder and smoother, moving towards a richer palate. The IGT Toscana Acciaiola is a blend of Sangiovese and Cabernet Sauvignon, and extends the style further in a more structured direction, but keeping that trademark freshness.

Castello Di Ama ★★★

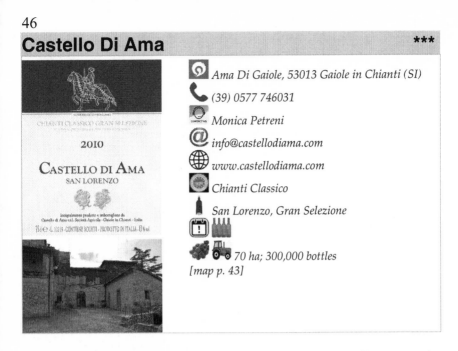

Ama Di Gaiole, 53013 Gaiole in Chianti (SI)

(39) 0577 746031

Monica Petreni

info@castellodiama.com

www.castellodiama.com

Chianti Classico

San Lorenzo, Gran Selezione

70 ha; 300,000 bottles

[map p. 43]

At the end of a long approach road, past the Vigneto Bellavista at the summit, Castello di Ama is in the hamlet of Ama. Some houses in the village are used for their restaurant and wine shop, and the winery is just to the side of the hamlet. The estate has 75 ha of vineyards (with 65 ha committed to Chianti Classico) and 35 ha of olive trees. Vineyards are between 390m and 530m altitude. The cellar was built in the eighties, and is full of stainless steel tanks for fermentation, and barriques for aging.

Founded in 1972, Castello di Ama released its first wine later in the decade. Today it is run by Lorenza Sebasti (second generation from one of the founding families) and her husband, winemaker Marco Pallanti. The focus here is on representing Chianti Classico by specific terroirs, all from locations in the vicinity of the winery. "We are in the highest part of the region," says Marco Pallanti. "The wine is different from the rest of Chianti, the altitude gives it freshness and a beautiful aroma. The second difference is the soil, it's very rich in calcareous stones, and this gives the minerality."

Before 2010, the only general estate Chianti Classico was the Riserva, but because vineyards were replanted, production was then split into two: Ama comes from vines under ten years old and basically representing the plantings of a new Sangiovese clone; San Lorenzo is a Gran Selezione that replaced the Riserva, and is a blend of 80% Sangiovese with 13% Merlot and 7% Malvasia Nera. ("Malvasia Nera is a good complement for Sangiovese, it is not so elegant, but it brings some spice.") There are two further Gran Selezione wines from single vineyards: Vigneto Bellavista

(82% Sangiovese and 18% Malvasia Nera) and Vigneto La Casuccia. (about 2 km to the north, less calcareous, with 80% Sangiovese and 20% Merlot; it is produced only in top vintages, eight times in the past twenty years).

The most famous wine here, however, may be the super-Tuscan l'Apparita. In 1982 Merlot was field grafted onto rootstocks in the Bellavista vineyard. "It was planted for blending in the Chianti, but the quality was so outstanding we decided to bottle it. This was the wine that made Ama famous," says Marco. Everything goes into barriques of French oak for 10-15 months. The Ama Chianti Classico goes into second and third year wood, San Lorenzo uses 30% new, and l'Apparita uses 40% new.

The style here goes from freshness in Ama, to weight in San Lorenzo, and elegance in Bellavista, where the lightness of the palate hides the underlying depth and potential for aging. Apparita is more like Bellavista than Bordeaux, with the mineral character of Ama coming right through In addition, Il Chiusa is an unusual blend of Sangiovese and Pinot Noir, which arose from a project to produce Pinot Noir. The latest wine is called Haiku "because it is a simple form but has meaning," Marco explains. It is half Sangiovese, and a quarter each Merlot and Cabernet Franc. It has the flavor spectrum of Sangiovese, but the texture of Bordeaux. An attractive feature of the wines is that all have moderate alcohol, in the range of 13-13.5%.

Marchesi Antinori *

Via Cassia per Siena, 133, 50026 Loc. Bargino, San Casciano in Val di Pesa (FI)

(39) 055 23595

Sara Nieddu

antinori@antinori.it

www.antinori.it

Chianti Classico

Badia a Passignano, Gran Selezione

330 ha; 1,700,000 bottles

[map p. 42]

The new Antinori winery in Chianti is a most impressive building. From a distance, it blends into the hillside as a long, thin line, which is not obvious to distinguish from the surroundings. From close up, it has striking swirls and curves, with a vineyard planted on the roof. Perhaps this is a metaphor for Antinori, which is one of Italy's most important wine producers, with eleven estates all over Italy. The new winery is the headquarters for administration as well as production. There are vast halls full of stainless steel fermentation tanks and barriques. Right opposite the grape reception center on the roof is a restaurant: the Marchesi is anxious that production should be as transparent as possible to visitors. The most important other estates are Tignanello (near by: see profile), Pian delle Vigne (in Montalcino: see profile), and Guado al Tasso (in Bolgheri: see profile).

There are four wines from Chianti Classico. After the basic Chianti Classico, there is Villa Antinori, which presents a traditionally tart view. A step up, the Marchesi Antinori Riserva used to come mostly from the Tignanello estate, supplemented by some other sources, but since 2011 has come exclusively from the Tignanello estate. "It matches Tignanello style more than Chianti Classico style," says winemaker Sara Pontemolesi, and today it is labeled as coming from Tenuta Tignanello. It is smoother and rounder than Villa Antinori.

"We consider Badia a Passignano to be our top Chianti Classico," Sara says. Now labeled as Gran Selezione (it used to be a Riserva), it comes from a 60 ha estate a few miles to the east, which makes only the Gran Selezione. Smooth and intense, when young it shows the Hungarian oak in which it is matured. "We think the French oak is too strong for Sangiovese. The aromatic notes of Hungarian oak are spicy, but do not have so much vanillin. The grain is not as fine as French, so they exchange better with the air. We don't want tannins so much as micro-oxygenation," Sara explains. Entirely Sangiovese, the style of Badia a Passignano is rich and chocolaty, well in the direction of Montalcino; in fact, the Rosso di Montalcino under the Antinori label is smooth and elegant, but with just a touch less intensity than the Badia a Passignano.

Outside of Tuscany, Antinori has an important estate in Umbria, Castello della Sala, which produces the IGT Cervara della Sala, a blend of Chardonnay with 10% Greccheto. "This is our top white wine, which started after the Marchesi went to Burgundy and asked why Italy could not produce a wine like Montrachet." The Greccheto brings acidity, which is needed as the wine does not go through MLF, and increases longevity: the wine has a strong mineral, smoky presence.

Badia A Coltibuono *

Badia a Coltibuono

VIN SANTO DEL CHIANTI CLASSICO

OCCHIO DI PERNICE

2003

📍 Località Badia a Coltibuono, 53013 Gaiole in Chianti (SI)

📞 (39) 0557 749498

Roberto Stucchi

@ info@coltibuono.com

🌐 www.coltibuono.com

Chianti Classico

🍷 Chianti Classico, Cultus Boni Riserva

🍷 Chianti Classico Vin Santo

☺ 🏭 ❌

🍇 🍂 63 ha; 240,000 bottles

[map p. 43]

Badia a Coltibuono was originally a monastery (founded by Benedictine monks in 1051); it expanded until 1810, when the monasteries were secularized. "It has been in our family since 1846," says Roberto Stucchi, who has been managing the estate since 1985. Today it houses a winery, boutique hotel, and restaurant (with a wine shop at the entrance to the access road that winds up to the hilltop at 630m). The buildings surround around a gracious courtyard, with a lovely ornamental garden behind. Wines are aged and stored in the extensive underground cellars, but the winery and vineyards are at Monti in Chianti, a few miles just to the south.

Production focuses on Sangiovese and other indigenous varieties. "I am going in the opposite direction from varietal wines," Roberto says. Chianti Classico and the Riserva are 90% Sangiovese with the other 10% coming from several indigenous varieties; there are no international varieties here. The Riserva is a selection of the best lots, chosen when the Chianti Classico is bottled. They are aged in 25 hl casks of Austrian or French oak. The Cultus Boni Riserva cuts Sangiovese back to 80%, and increases the number of indigenous varieties making up the rest: it is aged in barriques, including a little new oak. The latest addition to the range is Montebello, an IGT Toscana that is a blend from one barrel each of the various indigenous varieties. This sees more new oak. It comes from a vineyard containing old vines, which were used to provide material for planting the other vineyards. There is one monovarietal wine, Sangioveto, a 100% Sangiovese that comes from the oldest vines, but as though to mark the difference from Chianti Classico, it is labeled as a super-Tuscan.

The style is classic, moving from the fresh Chianti Classico to the Riserva, just a touch smoother, with notes of black as well as red fruits, showing the same focus on purity of fruits. Cultus Boni shows greater roundness and generosity, moving further towards black fruits. Sangioveto is the smoothest of the range, really showing the concentration of the old vines. Montebello shows as the most powerful wine. Of course, there's also Vin Santo, olive oils, and grappa. There also a separate range of wines, with the same total production as Badia a Coltibuono, but simply labeled Coltibuono, including Chianti, Chianti Classico, and IGT Toscana, from a negociant activity.

La Brancaia

Loc. *Poppo 42b, 53017 Radda in Chianti (SI)*

(39) 05777 42007

Barbara Widmer

brancaia@brancaia.it

www.brancaia.it

Chianti Classico

Chianti Classico Riserva

80 ha; 500,000 bottles

[map p. 43]

Brancaia is an unusual operation spanning Chianti to Maremma under one label; you have to look at the back label to see where the wine comes from. It started when Barbara Widmer's parents visited the Chianti region on holiday from Switzerland. They bought the Brancaia estate in 1980, and started to replant its 7 ha of vineyards. A couple of years later they bought the estate that is now their headquarters, at Poppi, and the grapes from the Brancaia and Poppi estates go into the same wine. Today there are 25 ha altogether in the Chianti region and since 1998 they have had an estate in Maremma with 48 ha.

Vineyards are not dedicated to any particular wine; "lots are assigned to wines depending on quality, so all the vineyards are farmed to the same level," Barbara explains. The entry-level wine, Tre, is a blend from Maremma and the Chianti region, Il Blu is a Merlot-Sangiovese blend from the Chianti region, and Illatria comes from Maremma. Illatria's first vintage was 2002, with a blend of 60% Cabernet Sauvignon, 30% Sangiovese, and 10% Petit Verdot. The blend changed dramatically in 2009 to 40% Cabernet Sauvignon, 40% Petit Verdot, and 20% Cabernet Franc. Production is 30,000 cases of Tre, 5-6,000 of Chianti Classico, 4,000 of Il Blu and 3-4,000 of Illatria. Wines are aged in either new or old barriques or tonneaux. "Any wine that isn't good enough to spend 12 months in wood isn't good enough for Brancaia," Barbara says. This is definitely a modernist producer.

Villa Cafaggio *

Via San Martino 5, 50020 Panzano In Chianti (FI)

(39) 0558 549094

Irene Cantini

info@cafaggio.wine

www.cafaggio.wine

Chianti Classico

Chianti Classico, Solatìo

30 ha; 200,000 bottles

[map p. 42]

Located below the town of Panzano in Chianti, Villa Cafaggio was a Benedictine monastery making wine in the Middle Ages. Its recent history is somewhat chequered. By the 1960s, when the Farkas family purchased it, the property had fallen into decay. It was restored and replanted, largely with Sangiovese, and in 1986 the first Cabernet vineyard was planted (by field grafting Cabernet over Canaiolo). The estate was purchased in 2005 by a cooperative from northern Italy (Cantina La-Vis e Valle di Cembra), but continued to function independently. It was sold in 2016 to the investment bank ISA.

Vineyards are all around, part of the Conca d'Or valley (named for the color of the cereal that used to be grown here). All 21 producers in the valley have agreed to make it entirely organic. The winery has an underground cellar built into the hillside in 1970 on two levels. A new barrel room is close by. Access to the winery is down a rather steep unpaved road; it would be better not to meet a truck coming the other way.

There are four Chianti Classicos and two IGTs. Chianti Classico comes from the estate and surrounding vineyards. The Riserva is a selection of the best estate grapes. Both are 100% Sangiovese and age in botti of Slavonian oak. There are two single vineyard wines in Chianti Classico: Solatìo and San Martino. Both are Riservas—"we don't understand Gran Selezione." Solatìo is 100% Sangiovese and ages in botti; San Martino has 85% Sangiovese, 10% Cabernet Sauvignon, and 5% Cabernet Franc, and ages in barriques (no new wood). The two "Crus" are IGT Toscana: Basilicata del Cortaccio is Cabernet Sauvignon, and Basilicata del Pruneto is Merlot. Both age in barriques.

A consistent style runs through the range from Chianti to IGTs. The Chianti Classico and the Riserva are quite close in style, both somewhat more generous than is usual for Chianti, but the Riserva has just a little more weight. Solatìo follows with more intensity, and San Martino marks a transition to a more modern style, more textured than Solatìo, somewhat of a halfway house to the international varieties of the IGTs. The vineyards for San Martino and Cortaccio are adjacent, and the wines show a surprising similarity of house style. At Villa Cafaggio they see the wines as developing in parallel, but say that the Sangiovese is a little more delicate, so may age faster if it is not a top year. San Martino's sense of granularity, almost chocolaty, intensifies in Cortaccio and Pruneto, which show a Tuscan take on the international varieties with the soft structure really underneath the fruit; Pruneto is more overt than Cortaccio.

Fattoria Di Fèlsina ***

Strada Chiantigiana S.San 484, 53019 Castelnuovo Berardenga (SI)

(39) 0577 355117

Giuseppe Mazzocolin

info@felsina.it

www.felsina.it

Chianti Classico

Chianti Classico Riserva, Rancia

94 ha; 480,000 bottles

[map p. 43]

One of the top properties in Chianti Classico, Fèlsina is located right at the southern border of the appellation. It's an extensive estate of about 150 ha, with olive trees as well as vineyards surrounded by forests. In fact, originally there were more olives than vines, and wine was made only for local consumption. The winery is located just on the edge of the town of Castelnuova Berardenga, and has an enoteca and tasting room. Fèlsina also owns Castello di Farnatella, an estate in Chianti Colli Senesi.

The estate was founded by Domenico Fèlsina in 1966, and today is run by his son-in-law, Giuseppe Mazzocolin, who still shows his origins as a professor of philosophy. Giuseppe believes in Sangiovese. "In 1983 I started to make wine 100% of Sangiovese." In the old vineyards there were Colorino, Trebbiano, and Malvasia, but replanting has used only Sangiovese, all sourced from selection massale with "probably about 30 subvarieties." Giuseppe's motto for production is "never too much," which applies to oak, extract, and so on, and no doubt explains the finesse of the wines. Giuseppe brings the same keen analysis to bear on his production of olive oil as on his Chianti: a visit to Felsina is incomplete without a tasting of the four monovarietal olive oils. "Olives vary with variety, terroir, vintage, but not as much as the grape," Giuseppe says.

The Chianti Classico Berardenga comes from a variety of vineyards in the estate, and is matured in Slavonian oak, with a small percentage in small barrels. The Berardenga Riserva is a selection and uses 30% French barriques. The Rancia Riserva comes from a vineyard at 350m elevation around the old Rancia farmhouse at the northern border of the property, and is matured for 20 months in 2-3-year-old French oak. Fontalloro is labeled as IGT Toscana because it comes from three vineyards, one at a high elevation within the Chianti Classico part of the estate, two others at lower elevation over the border into Chianti Colli Senesi. It's vinified in a mix of new and one-year French barriques. Colonia is a Chianti Classico from a 2 ha vineyard at the highest point in the property, 400m (planted in 1993). Made only in top years, it started as an IGT in 2006 and 2007, then became Gran Selezione in 2009; when Colonia is not made, the grapes are declassified to Rancia. It is aged for 24 months in barriques, including new oak. I Sistri is a Chardonnay labeled as IGT Toscana. Maestro Raro is a 100% Cabernet Sauvignon, and the most powerful of Fèlsina's wines..

The style here ranges from traditional to modernist. The most traditional wine is the Chianti Classico Berardenga, which shows classic freshness. Rancia Riserva and Fontalloro place at the same price point in the range, but Fontalloro is more powerful, more chocolaty, than Rancia, which has more of the classic freshness. The same relationship holds through warm and cool vintages. The Gran Selezione Colonia actually has more oak exposure than Fontalloro, but shows it less obviously. While Fontalloro is an expression of modern Chianti, tending towards the power of (say) Brunello, Colonia is the finest of the cuvées, and has a more traditional typicity, even though it ages in new barriques.

Castello Di Fonterutoli

**

🔵 *Via Ottone III di Sassonia 5, Loc. Fonterutoli, 53011 Castellina In Chianti (SI)*

📞 *(39) 0577 735757*

👤 *Filippo Mazzei*

@ *mazzei@mazzei.it*

🌐 *www.fonterutoli.it*

⬤ *Chianti Classico*

🍾 *Chianti Classico Riserva, Ser Lapo*

😊 🍷 ❌

🍇 ⏱ *117 ha; 800,000 bottles*

[map p. 43]

The Fonterutoli estate came into the Mazzei family by marriage in 1398. Some 24 generations later, the Mazzei estates include Fonterutoli, Belguardo in Maremma, and Zisola in Sicily. At the southern border of Chianti Classico, the Castello is located in a hamlet dating more or less from the sixteenth century, and close enough to Siena to see the city on the horizon. The estate covers 650 ha, with vineyards a little under 20%. The vineyards form 120 separate parcels, at elevations varying from 220 to 550 m, with soils based on Alberese and sandstone, but basically fall into five groups based on elevation and soils.

Everything is vinified by parcel and tasted before making the blends. "The blend is always more complex than the individual wines," says Filippo Mazzei. All the Chiantis are blends of different varieties. There is some pressure to make 100% Sangiovese, but Filippo does not think this is necessary. "It is simplistic to believe that 100% Sangiovese is necessarily best for keeping typicity." The Chianti Classico is called simply Fonterutoli, and is blend of 90% Sangiovese with Malvasia Nera and Colorino, aged in a mix of barriques and tonneau, about 40% new. "We changed from botti to barriques around 1996 because the Sangiovese with new clones, high density, basically lower yields and more concentration, needs more oxidative exposure," says winemaker Luca Biffa.

The Riserva is the Ser Lapo, which includes Merlot and Cabernet Sauvignon, and is aged exclusively in barriques (half new), and there is also a Ser Lapo Riserva Privata made in small amounts. The Gran Selezione (formerly a Riserva), which comes from a selection of the best vineyards, is called Castello Fonterutoli; it's a similar blend to Fonterutoli but also includes some Merlot, and is similarly aged in a mix of French barriques and tonneaux, with about 60% new wood.

Fonterutoli is one of the relatively few producers where the best grapes are taken for the Riserva, which is the top wine, as opposed to a super-Tuscan IGT. "If your top wine is a Sangiovese, it should be in the DOC," Filippo says. There are three super-Tuscans. Siepi comes from the Siepi vineyard and is an equal blend of Sangiovese and Merlot, aged in oak barriques with 70% new; Concerto is a blend of 80% Sangiovese with 20% Cabernet Sauvignon; and the most recent is Mix36, a 100% Sangiovese from 36 different cultivars planted ten years ago. Twelve are clones, the rest chosen by selection massale, "not necessarily from Tuscany, in fact three of our best clones come from Romania," says Filippo.

Fontodi   ***

⊙ *Località Fontodi San Leolino, 50020 Panzano in Chianti (FI)*

📞 *(39) 0558 52005*

Giovanni Manetti

@ *fontodi@fontodi.com*

🌐 *www.fontodi.com*

◉ *Chianti Classico*

🍾 *Vigna del Sorbo, Gran Selezione*

🙂 🏭

🍇 🍇 *80 ha; 300,000 bottles*

[map p. 43]

Originally involved in producing terracotta tiles in the region, the Manetti family moved into wine production in 1968. The winery sits in a commanding position looking out over the amphitheater of the valley, where the 130 ha estate includes a more or less contiguous array of vineyards and a farm. Agriculture is organic, and largely self-sustaining, with manure from the 25 cows at the farm used for the vineyards.

The Chiantis have been aged in barriques since 1980. "French oak softens the astringency of Sangiovese; I would prefer to see people using French barriques to soften the wine rather than using 20% international varieties," says Giovanni Manetti. However, Giovanni is experimenting with returning to botti, and also with amphorae, made by his brother at the family tile factory. The Chianti Classico is aged in old French barriques. The Vigna del Sorbo Gran Selezione (formerly Riserva) comes from the del Sorbo vineyard and is aged in barriques with half new.

When Vigna del Sorbo was introduced in 1985, it contained 10% Cabernet Sauvignon; since then the vineyard has been replanted, and a parcel of 45-year-old vines was added in 2009, bringing the Cabernet proportion down to 5% today. Giovanni thinks that blending Sangiovese with other varieties can be overdone. "It is not a mistake to allow other varieties, but if the official limit is 20%, it should be enforced. The recent change from 15% to 20% was a mistake. Some wines have been embarrassing in the past, showing black fruits rather than red fruits."

Fontodi's top wine is Flaccianello della Pieve, a selection of 100% Sangiovese from the best vineyards, labeled as Toscana IGT. Other IGTs include the Cabernet Sauvignon Meriggio, the Syrah Casa Via, and the Pinot Noir Case Via. Why is the top wine an IGT when it could be a Chianti Classico? "It's not the right moment yet to go back to the Chianti name. I'd like to see a trade in which the best wines return to Chianti DOC in return for a better classification system that distinguishes the communes."

Marchesi de Frescobaldi   *

Castello Nipozzano, Località Nipozzano Fattoria, 50060 Nipozzano (FI)

(39) 055 27141

info@frescobaldi.it

www.frescobaldi.it

Chianti Rufina

IGT Toscana, Montesodi

1200 ha; 10,000,000 bottles

[map p. 42]

The Frescobaldis were bankers in medieval Florence, and have been involved with producing wine for seven centuries. Today the wines are produced by Lamberto Frescobaldi. To say that Frescobaldi is a large producer is an understatement: focused on Tuscany, there are six estates: Tenuta Castiglioni (the original estate at Monterspertoli to the west of Chianti Classico, which produces the Giramonte IGT), Castello Nipozzano (Chianti Rufina), Castello Pomino (east of Florence, producing a variety of wines under the Pomino DOC), Tenuta Castelgioconda (in Montalcino and also producing a super-Tuscan), and Rèmole (IGT wines) and Tenuta Ammiraglia (Magiono in Maremma). Their most prestigious holding, however, is Ornellaia, in Bolgheri.

In terms of Sangiovese, the main offerings come from Nipozzano and Castelgioconda. (Chianti Classico is a notable gap in the portfolio.) There's a step up in quality from the Nipozzano Riserva, a Chianti Rufina which includes international varieties but can be a little hard, to the Vecchia Vita, which has only indigenous varieties and comes from the oldest plantings at Nipozzano. Both bring out the classic sour red cherry fruits.

Montesodi is a monovarietal Sangiovese from the named vineyard on the Nipozzano estate that shows its antecedents by bringing out the fresh character of the variety, and then Ripe al Convento is a single vineyard wine from Castelgioconda, more or less at the same 400m elevation as Montesodi, but giving a riper impression with more fruit intensity. Comparison between Montesodi, which might be considered analogous to a Chianti Classico Gran Selezione, and Ripe al Convento is somewhat indicative of the general difference between Chianti and Brunello di Montalcino. Close to Castelgioconda, but separate from it, the Luce della Vite estate is Frescobaldi's high end in Montalcino (see profile), producing the super-Tuscan Luce, a blend of Sangiovese and Merlot, its second wine, Lucente, and more recently also a Brunello (from 5 of the 77 ha of the estate).

I Sodi

*

Loc. I Sodi, Frazione Monti, 53013 Gaiole in Chianti (SI)

(39) 0577 747012

Andrea Casini

info@agrisodi.com

www.agrisodi.com

Chianti Classico

Chianti Classico Riserva

Chianti Classico Vin Santo

12 ha; 90,000 bottles

[map p. 43]

The name of the estate means hard ground, referring to the stony soil. A very long approach leads from the main road to the somewhat isolated property; from the winery you can see the Castle of Brolio on the hills in the distance. The estate had been more or less abandoned until the Casini family purchased it in 1973 and planted 9 ha of vineyards and 3 ha of olive groves. "My grandfather bought the property from the Church to make wine for the family because he didn't think much of the quality of Chianti at the time," says Andrea Cassini, who manages the estate today. Vineyards surround the property and face south, but although this is a warm spot, it is kept fresh by an underground spring. The cellar built in 1982 was extended in 2007.

The entry level wine here is an IGT Toscana, Solerto, which has a blend of traditional varieties: Sangiovese, Canaiolo, Malvasia Nera, and Trebbiano. The Chianti Classicos are blends of Sangiovese and Canaiolo, with a big step up from Chianti Classico to the Riserva, which is a selection of the best grapes in the best years, and is not produced every year. Soprasassi is an unusual monovarietal of Canaiolo, which shows a surprising sense of completeness, in the typical savory flavor spectrum of the region. The top wine is Vigna Farsina, a monovarietal Sangiovese. Why is it an IGT and not Chianti Classico? "Because the volume is very small. We already have a Riserva. We could have made a Gran Selezione, but I think many Gran Seleziones are Riserva relabeled, we wanted to do something new." With an impression of umami and gunflint, it is in fact the very model of a modern Chianti Classico.

The Chianti Classico ages in Slavonian botti; the Riserva, Soprasassi and Farsina age in barriques. The style is modern and elegant, although eschewing international varieties. Going from the Riserva to the Vigna Farsina, there's an increasingly silky sheen, which shows even in the monovarietal Canaiolo. The Vin Santo—"we produce a true Vin Santo," says Andrea—comes from grapes that dry for 3-4 months in a loft, and the wine ages for 6 years in 50-150 liter casks. It has a delicious sweet/sour balance with a mineral edge, and indeed is the real thing.

Isole E Olena   **

Loc. Isole, 1, 50021 Barberino Val d'Elsa (FI)

(39) 0558 072763

Marta De Marchi

isolena@tin.it

www.isoleolena.it

Chianti Classico

IGT Toscana, Cepparello

Chianti Classico Vin Santo

50 ha; 200,000 bottles [map p. 43]

Perched at the end of a path half way up a mountain, Isole is where the winery is located, and below is the hamlet of Olena, whose occupants used to survive by sharecropping the land. The estate was formed when Paolo de Marchi's father combined two properties in 1956, one in Isole and one in Olena. The soils are galestro. He was thinking of selling it when Paolo came from Piedmont in 1976 and decided to create the vineyards. (Paolo now makes a Nebbiolo from the old family vineyards in Lessona under the name of Proprietà Sperino.)

Paolo is a forceful character who bubbles over with ideas and goes his own way. Explaining why his top wine, Ceparello remains an IGT Toscana although it is 100% Sangiovese, he says, "Wine of origin to me is not anymore in the appellation. Everything in the appellation works for brands and not for the real origin. They certify the provenance but that is not enough." Ceparello is a selection of the best lots of Sangiovese and is aged in French barriques. The Chianti Classico is a blend of 80% Sangiovese with Canaiolo and Syrah. "The pressure to make Chianti just from Sangiovese is taking things to excess. What is Chianti—since it has always been a blend, of course the nature of that blend will change with time." The Gran Selezione has small amounts of Cabernet, Syrah, and Petit Verdot, but stays true to Chianti's freshness.

The Isole e Olena label alone is used for traditional wines based on Sangiovese, while Collezione De Marchi is used for other varieties and includes Chardonnay, Syrah, and Cabernet Sauvignon. The Cabernet Sauvignon comes from a vineyard that was originally planted with the intention of improving the Chianti Classico; but Paolo decided that Cabernet would overwhelm the Sangiovese. "I don't like trying to use blending to improve poor results, as opposed to putting complementary varieties together to increase complexity," he says. The Cabernet also includes a little Cabernet Franc and Petit Verdot.

Paoli is somewhat sceptical about the DOCG classification system, but says, "There is a sort of de facto classification of estates, with people recognizing the quality producers." It is widely recognized that in any such classification, Isole e Olena would be in the top tier.

Il Molino Di Grace *

Località Il Volano, Panzano in Chianti (FI)

(39) 0558 561010

Tim Grace

info@ilmolinodigrace.it

www.ilmolinodigrace.com

Chianti Classico

Chianti Classico Riserva

44 ha

[map p. 43]

There have been vineyards here for three centuries. The name refers to both an old windmill (Molino) on the property, and the current owners, the Grace family, who purchased the property in 1995. Grapes had previously been sold to local producers, but an abandoned nineteenth century ruin was renovated to become the winery, and the first vintage was 1999. There are three Chiantis: Classico, Classico Riserva, and Gran Selezione. All are 100% Sangiovese, the first two matured in wood casks of various sizes, the Gran Selezione in barriques and tonneaux with some new oak. It's not a criticism of the Riserva to say that it shows only a touch more depth than the Classico *tout court,* but is rather a comment on the unusual smoothness and ripeness of the simple Chianti Classico. The Gran Selezione retains the freshness of Chianti. Coming from vines more than 55 years old, IGT Toscana Gratius is more traditional in its grape varieties than the Chiantis, with very small amounts of Canaiolo and Colorino as well as Sangiovese, but with a significant amount of new oak, it shows a more international character. Another IGT, Il Volano, is three quarters Sangiovese and a quarter Merlot.

Castello Di Monsanto

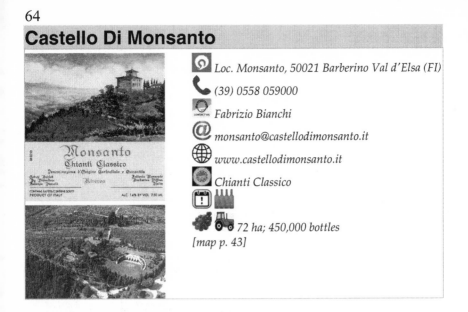

Loc. Monsanto, 50021 Barberino Val d'Elsa (FI)

(39) 0558 059000

Fabrizio Bianchi

monsanto@castellodimonsanto.it

www.castellodimonsanto.it

Chianti Classico

72 ha; 450,000 bottles
[map p. 43]

Located in the northern part of Chianti, this is one of the most charming estates in the region, with a view over to the towers of San Gimignano. It was founded when Aldo Bianchi bought the property in 1960; today it is run by his son Fabrizio. The entry level wine is a Chianti DOCG, Monrosso, which comes from the Colli Senesi area. The three Chianti Classicos are quite traditional in their constitution, with a blend of 90% Sangiovese and small amounts of Canaiolo and Colorino. The Chianti Classico matures in 50 hl barrels of Slavonian oak, the Riserva ages in small wooden barrels, and the Il Poggio Riserva, produced only in top vintages, matures in French barriques. The Toscana IGTs are labeled as Fabrizio Bianchi, and include the Rosato, which is a second wine from young vines, a Sangiovese, and a Chardonnay. Nemo is a monovarietal Cabernet Sauvignon.

Montevertine ✱✱

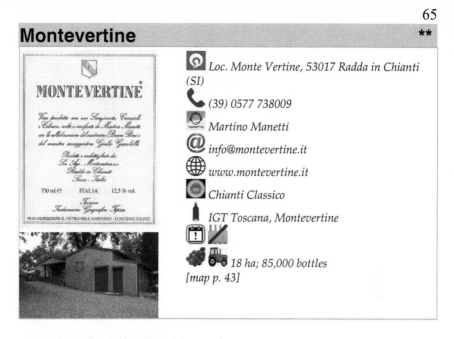

Loc. *Monte Vertine, 53017 Radda in Chianti (SI)*

(39) 0577 738009

Martino Manetti

info@montevertine.it

www.montevertine.it

Chianti Classico

IGT Toscana, Montevertine

18 ha; 85,000 bottles

[*map p. 43*]

Located in the hills of Radda in Chianti, Montevertine is a famous producer who actually produces no Chianti Classico. The three wines are the eponymous Montevertine, Pian del Ciampolo, and Le Pergole Torte, all labeled as IGT Toscana. Sergio Manetti acquired Montevertine in 1967 as a vacation. He planted a small vineyard in order to make some wine for the family, but this was so successful soon he became a full time wine producer. Because he would not use Trebbiano in his blend, he was refused the Chianti Classico label; so he left the Consorzio, and never returned. The irony is that Montevertine is a rare producer in the area who has never taken up the international varieties, but has stayed true to Chianti's traditions.

Today the estate is run by Sergio's son, Martino. "My father always wanted to focus on Sangiovese without planting international grapes. I promised my father never to return to the Consorzio," he says. The winery is a cluster of small buildings perched on top of a hill at the end of a narrow, precipitous approach road. It's very hands-on: Martino was in the cellars pumping-over several tanks when I visited. Production is increasing a little as a result of planting a new vineyard, but will not increase any further. "I have no more room in the cellar. Going over 100,000 bottles would change everything radically, I want to go on doing everything without outside help."

The vineyards, with 11 ha on the hill around the winery and another 7 ha a few miles away in the same valley, are dedicated exclusively to traditional varieties: Sangiovese, Colorino, and Canaiolo. "There are only three red wines, they are different but they can be considered as brothers," says Martino. Pian del Ciampolo is effectively a second wine to Montevertine, which is the first selection. Both are around 90% Sangiovese, and are aged in the traditional large casks of Slavonian oak, Ciampolo for one year and Montevertine for two years.

Exclusively Sangiovese, the prestige cuvée Le Pergole Torte comes from the first vineyard that Sergio planted, just at the entrance to the property. The vineyard has been extended a bit, but 60% of the vines are the original stock. "It was the first 100% Sangiovese made in this area, I remember many people coming to taste, they were surprised to find something new in Chianti," Martino recollects. It is aged in French barriques (10-15% new). (There used to be a fourth wine, Il Sodaccio, but this ceased production when the vineyard had to be replanted.) Part of the elegance is the moderate alcohol. "This is the coolest area in all Chianti Classico, we're high up, sometimes it's hard to get 12%, the most we ever had was 14% in 2011," Martino says. Always running through the wines here, there is a savory acidity, with a sense of minerality, reaching its peak in Le Pergole Torte, which is regarded by many as the epitome of Sangiovese. Montevertine and Le Pergole Torte age beautifully, becoming increasingly subtle with time.

Tenuta di Nozzole ✱

🔘 *Via di Nozzole 12, Loc, Passo Dei Pecora, 50020 Greve in Chianti (FI)*

📞 *(39) 0558 59811*

👤 *Giovanni Mazzoni*

@ *folonari@tenutefolonari.com*

🌐 *www.tenuteambrogioegiovannifolonari.com*

🔴 *Chianti Classico*

🍾 *IGT Toscana, Il Pareto*

🍾 *IGT Toscana, La Bruniche*

⬛🍷🍇🚜 *100 ha*

[map p. 42]

Nozzole has a slightly chequered history. Located in the northern part of the Chianti area, there have been vineyards here for several hundred years. The Folonaris, who moved into Chianti to make a transition to quality wine at the start of the twentieth century, purchased the estate in 1971. (They owned Ruffino, and introduced the famous Chianti straw flasks). In 2000, the company was divided, and Ambrogio Folonari and his son Giovanni kept Nozzole and Cabreo, near Greve in Chianti. They also started Campo al Mare in Bolgheri, as well as La Fuga in Montalcino, Torcalvano in Montepulciano, and Vigne a Porrona in Maremma. Altogether there are seven estates in their portfolio.

Nozzole produces Chianti Classico, Le Bruniche Chardonnay, and the Il Pareto monovarietal Cabernet Sauvignon. The style is modern, with the wines aged in barriques, and flavors tending towards fruity rather than savory. "This area gives richer rounder wines than the usual austere Chianti," says winemaker Roberto. From the Cabreo vineyards there are La Pietra Chardonnay and Il Borgo, a blend of 30% Cabernet Sauvignon with 70% Sangiovese. "The soul of Tuscany, Sangiovese, is fruit driven with high acidity; we wanted to combine it with the power of Cabernet Sauvignon to give structure and longevity," says Roberto. The varietal composition is more determinative of style here than the vineyard characters, since Il Pareto is sandier and lower, while Cabreo has rocky soil at higher altitude; but with 100% Cabernet, Il Pareto is a bigger wine than Cabreo. "But Il Pareto became too powerful, and we eased back around 2008 (using some tonneaux instead of barriques) to look for more elegance," says Roberto. Il Pareto is very much the Chianti-centric view of Cabernet Sauvignon, savory and elegant, a match for food.

Panzanello *

Loc. Panzanello, Via Case Sparse, 86, 50022 Panzano in Chianti (FI)

(39) 0558 52470

Andrea Sommaruga

info@panzanello.it

www.panzanello.it

Chianti Classico

Chianti Classico Riserva

14 ha; 50,000 bottles
[map p. 42]

"I am not a traditionalist, I am not a modernist, I am myself," says Andrea Sommaruga, who came to make wine on this estate in 1994. His grandmother, who lived in Rome and wanted a property in Tuscany, bought this old estate in 1964. "I was previously in finance, I knew nothing about wine. I came here thinking it would be a relaxed business, but in the summer I was here working, and in the winter I had to sell the wine. I started with 8,000 bottles of the 1995 vintage in 1997, 12,000 the year after. But most of the grapes were sold to the coop: my grandmother was one of the founders. I cancelled the contract with the coop in 1998. We bought some more land and planted new vineyards in 1999." The facilities have been expanded with a new cellar and tasting room, and several apartments for accommodation on site. It's a very hands-on operation, with Andrea and Ioletta Sommaruga living in a villa on the 120 ha estate.

There are four wines. The Chianti Classico includes a small proportion of Merlot and is aged used 500 liter barrels. The Riserva is a selection from the best vineyards, has some Cabernet Sauvignon, and is aged in one-year-old oak. The IGT Toscana Il Manuzio is based on a selection of the best lots of Sangiovese and Merlot, and is aged in new barriques. "This is my baby," says Andrea. It's not made every year: first in 2010 and then in 2014. Vindea is Ioletta's project, an equal combination of Sangiovese and Petit Verdot, started in 2006 with the next vintage in 2011. "The IGTs are our top wines, absolutely, but in terms of making Chianti Classico, the Riserva is absolutely the top wine. We don't believe in Gran Selezione, absolutely not."

A powerful house style is evident at once in the deep colors, and the black fruit spectrum of the palates, with the impression of structure increasing as you go along the series; although it remains relatively subtle, fruits become less overt. Chianti Classico shows forward fruits, while the Riserva is deeper, yet more restrained with an impression of minerality. Il Manuzio increases the sense of spicy structure and more reserve to the fruits. Vindea is the most powerful wine and needs time to develop. The olive oil is also quite powerful and peppery.

Castello Di Querceto

***

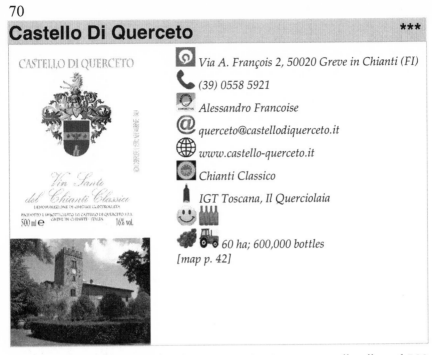

Via A. François 2, 50020 Greve in Chianti (FI)

(39) 0558 5921

Alessandro Francoise

querceto@castellodiquerceto.it

www.castello-querceto.it

Chianti Classico

IGT Toscana, Il Querciolaia

60 ha; 600,000 bottles

[map p. 42]

The sixteenth century castle of Querceto dominates a small valley of 500 ha where vineyards were first planted in 1897 by Alessandro François's grandfather. Alessandro was an engineer in Milan and moved here to run the vineyards in 1983. Today, Querceto has about 250 ha of vineyards, at elevations of 400-500m; in this slightly cooler climate, harvest is generally a couple of weeks after others in the region. "We have three different areas in the valley, with very different soil types, this is why we decided to produce single vineyard wines," says Alessandro.

There are four super-Tuscans. La Corte is a single vineyard Sangiovese. "It started as an experiment. One hundred years ago my grandfather planted the first vineyard of 100% Sangiovese. This was the first single vineyard wine—our first super-Tuscan in 1904," says Alessandro. Il Querciolaia is a blend of Sangiovese and Cabernet Sauvignon ("We tried 50% Cabernet, the Sangiovese disappeared, we tried 10-15% it was not enough, so we decided about 30%"); Cignale is a Cabernet Sauvignon with just a softening of 10% Merlot; and Il Sole di Alessandro is a monovarietal Cabernet Sauvignon. "When we started to produce international varieties our idea was to find the maximum link between the varieties and the terroir," explains Alessandro.

There is also, of course, a Chianti Classico. This is traditional: "I produce Chianti Classico without an international variety because in my opinion it must retain the character of the past." Querceto's wines are, in my opinion, among the most elegant of the Chianti Classico region.

Querciabella ***

Via Barbiano 17, 50022 Greve in Chianti (FI)

(39)055 8592 7732

Roberto Lasorte

info@querciabella.com

www.querciabella.com

Chianti Classico

Chianti Classico

IGT Toscana, Batàr

101 ha; 330,000 bottles

[map p. 42]

Querciabella started as a hobby in 1974 but rapidly became a fully professional producer. Located up a dirt track on a mountainside just outside of Greve in Chianti, the estate became organic in 1988, and biodynamic in 2000. There is also an estate of 35 ha in Maremma. The last few years have seen intensive modernization, with new facilities constructed to allow more precise control of production, including vinification plot by plot. More than 90% of the plantings are Sangiovese.

The estate presently produces four wines: Chianti Classico (100% Sangiovese since 2010: "the Sangiovese has now improved to the point at which is doesn't need the added strength of Cabernet," says winemaker Manfred Ing); the Batàr blend of Pinot Blanc and Chardonnay (named to indicate its intended relationship with great Burgundy); the Palafreno monovarietal Merlot (made only in the best vintages, which are not necessarily the warmest); and Camartina, a blend of 70% Cabernet Sauvignon and 30% Sangiovese. Mongrana, a blend of Sangiovese, Merlot, and Cabernet Sauvignon, comes from a 30 hectare estate at Maremma. There is increasing emphasis here on terroir, with plans to introduce single vineyard wines, although one recent cuvée goes in the opposite direction: Turpino is an IGT blend of Cabernet Franc, Syrah and Merlot, composed of equal proportions of grapes from Chianti and Maremma. The style here is firm and elegant.

Castello Dei Rampolla ★★

⊙ *Via San Lucia In Faulle, 50020 Panzano in Chianti (FI)*

☎ *(39) 0558 52533*

✉ *Maurizia di Napoli Rampolla*

@ *castellodeirampolla.cast@tin.it*

⊕ *www.castellodeirampolla.it*

◉ *Chianti Classico*

▮ *Chianti Classico Riserva*

⬛ ⫼

🍇 ◯ *32 ha; 80,000 bottles*
[map p. 42]

This thirteenth century estate has been owned by the Di Napoli family since 1739. During the 1960s the Rampolla estate was mostly olive trees, and Alceo di Napoli sold grapes to Antinori. Today the estate, just below the town of Panzano-in-Chianti, is mostly covered in vineyards. Basically four wines are made here, two based on Sangiovese and two based on Cabernet Sauvignon. "We started planting Cabernet Sauvignon in the late seventies, the intention was to blend it to reinforce the Sangiovese. We took out the Malvasia, Trebbiano, and Canaiolo. We wanted to make a wine that would stand by itself. It was going to be a Chianti, but it wasn't quite legal," recollects Luca di Napoli, who runs the estate together with his sister. The Chianti Classico includes 5% each of Cabernet Sauvignon and Merlot, and a 100% Sangiovese IGT Toscana, matured in terracotta amphorae without any sulfur was introduced in 2010. The blend for Sammarco, one of the first super-Tuscans, which started with the 1980 vintage, is the opposite of the Chianti, with 80% Cabernet Sauvignon to the minority of Merlot and Sangiovese. Vigna d'Alceo is a blend of 85% Cabernet Sauvignon with 15% Petit Verdot. The two wines are somewhat representative of two styles of super-Tuscan: the first tending towards elegance and almost savory; the second showing more direct fruits and power in a more international style.

Barone Ricasoli *

Cantine Del Castello Di Brolio, 53010 Gaiole in Chianti (SI)

(39) 0577 7301

Simona Brandini

barone@ricasoli.it

www.ricasoli.it

Chianti Classico

Colledila, Gran Selezione

235 ha; 2,000,000 bottles

[map p. 43]

Barone Ricasoli claims to be the oldest winery in Italy, making wine at the Castelo di Brolio since 1141. The eponymous Baron was involved in the establishment of Chianti, and famously devised the first formula for the varietal mix in 1872. The estate has been run since 1993 by Francesco Ricasoli, the 32nd Baron of Brolio, after a somewhat chequered history in the previous decades. As the result of financial difficulties, the winery and brand were sold to Seagrams in 1953, and then Seagrams sold it on to a British businessman in 1986. Seagrams more or less wrecked the business, as it ruined every other wine estate it acquired. The vineyards continued to be owned by the Ricasolis, but could not be well maintained because grapes had to be sold by contract to Seagrams at a low price. In 1993, Francesco was able to buy back the winery and brand name.

The Brolio winery is the largest in Chianti, surrounded by an estate of 1,200 ha that extends from Gaiole in Chianti to Castelnuova Berardenga. It includes 26 ha of olive groves as well as 235 ha of vineyards. Soon after he took over, Francesco replanted the vineyards at higher density, with blocks of each variety replacing the previously intermingled plantings. The cellars were renovated and extended, and now form a vast expanse around and underneath a large courtyard. Basically everything—cellars and vineyards—have been renewed since 1997.

Continuing the tradition of research, Ricasoli has been involved with the development of clones of Sangiovese. "The estate has always been at the front of advancing things in Chianti and we like to feel we can do that today. We are one of the largest estates but we are not comparable to the industrial producers," Francesco says. With such a large estate there are several types of terroir, including sandstone, galestro, and limestone. There is a wide range of wines. The estate Chianti Classico and Riserva have 20% Merlot and Cabernet Sauvignon, but Brolio-Bettino pays respect to tradition with a Sangiovese-Colorino blend matured only in large old casks. Two Gran Selezione wines demonstrate the two faces of the company. Colledila is a 100% Sangiovese single vineyard wine coming from a 7 ha vineyard with calcareous soils, while Castelo di Brolio is based on selection of the best lots of Sangiovese with small amounts of Cabernet Sauvignon and Petit Verdot. The IGT Toscanas include the 100% Merlot Casalferro (based on selecting the best 4 ha from a 10 ha vineyard with sandstone and limestone soils) and the Chardonnay-Sauvignon blend of Terricello. Sangiovese is usually aged in tonneaux—"we like the micro-oxygenation," says winemaker Massimiliano Biagi, and international varieties are aged in barriques.

The Chianti Classico and Riserva show the fresh style of Sangiovese, Colledila is a chic, elegant version of the savory side of Sangiovese, Castelo shows the modern face of Chianti Classico, and Casalferro is a Tuscan take on Merlot. The trend is now towards showcasing different terroirs: "Sangiovese wines representing different soils will be a feature of the 2015 vintage. We started this approach more than ten years ago, but so far we have released only one wine. If you are 100% Sangiovese, the message comes through more clearly. But we also made a Cru that is pure Merlot, it shows how it can be Tuscan, Chiantified if you like," Francesco says. Ricasoli remains a driving force in Chianti Classico. The castle and is gardens are one of the sights of the region; there's an expansive tasting room, and also a restaurant in the castle.

Rocca Delle Macìe

**

Localitá Le Macìe, 53011 Castellina in Chianti (SI)

(39) 0577 743220

Thomas Francioni

rocca@roccadellemacie.com

www.roccadellemacie.com

Chianti Classico

Fizzano, Gran Selezione

150 ha; 3,000,000 bottles
[map p. 43]

The estate was founded in 1973, when film producer Italo Zingarelli purchased the property, which at the time had only 2 ha of vines. The buildings around the main courtyard are now residential or used for hospitality; the large modern winery is below on one side. The original cellar from 1973 now houses a dozen botti, and seems awfully small compared with today's operation, which is one of the largest producers in Chianti Classico. From the original Le Macìe property, wine production has expanded into other estates, including Sant'Alfonso and Fizzano, also in Chianti Classico, and Campomaccione and Casamaria in Morellino di Scansano. The combined estates include 80 ha of olive trees as well as the vineyards. Italo's son Sergio has been running the company since 1985, and is presently Chairman of the Consorzio del Chianti Classico.

The range of fourteen wines includes several from Chianti Classico, including a series carrying the Zingarelli name, forming the range Chianti Classico Famiglia Zingarelli, Riserva Famiglia Zingarelli, and Gran Selezione Sergio Zingarelli, which is the most recent cuvée. "This is a limited production and would have been an IGT Toscana if the Gran Selezione category had not been created," says Sergio. The other estates are represented by a Chianti Classico from Sant'Alfonso and a Gran Selezione from Fizzano (named the Riserva di Fizzano, this has now become a Gran Selezione). "We like to have wines that come from the individual estates," says marketing manager Thomas Francioni. The Chianti Classico ages in 100 hl Slavonian botti, the Riserva in a 36 hl French casks, and the Gran Seleziones age in a mixture of large and small casks. Besides Chianti, there are several super-Tuscans, including two Sangiovese-Cabernet blends, Roccato and Ser Gioveto, and a Sangiovese-Merlot blend, Rubizzo. Many other DOCs are represented in the range, including Brunello di Montal-cino, Montepulciano, and Bolgheri.

The entry-level Chianti Classico, which is a blend from all the terroirs, has a fresh pungent style; then the rest of the range gives a smooth, rounded impression. "I want elegance, elegance, elegance, not power," says Sergio. Going up the series, that sense of smoothness doesn't change so much as the sense of accompanying texture. although palate weight increases, but there is always that touch of minerality and gunflint at the end to remind you of the dominance of Sangiovese. The super-Tuscans follow the same style, with Ser Gioveto following the lines of Sergio Zinga-relli, more Sangiovese-dominated, and Roccato, which is moving towards greater Cabernet and a more Bordeaux-like impression, showing more ob-vious structure at the expense of opulence. A consistent view of Sangiovese comes across the whole range.

Rocca di Castagnoli   *

Loc. *Castagnoli, 53010 Gaiole in Chianti (SI)*

(39) 0577 731004

Rolando Bernacchini

info@roccadicastagnoli.com

www.roccadicastagnoli.com

Chianti Classico

Chianti Classico Riserva, a'Frati

IGT Toscana, Il Buriano

132 ha; 500,000 bottles
[map p. 43]

Wine has been made around the medieval village of Castagnoli for several hundred years. The Castagnoli estate was well known in the eighteenth century, at the end of the nineteenth century it passed into the hands of the Ricasolis, in 1981 it was purchased by Calogero Calì, who subsequently purchased several other wine estates, including Tenuta di Capraia in Chianti, Poggio Maestrino-Spiaggiole in Maremma, and Poggio Graffetta in Sicily; the holding company is called Alimenta. Rocca di Castagnoli has 850 ha, with 15 ha of olive groves as well as the vineyards, and includes a historical house that has been converted into a hotel. After a research program, specific clones of Sangiovese were developed that are now used for planting the vineyards.

The Chianti Classico is a blend of Sangiovese, Colorino, and Canaiolo matured in a mixture of casks and tonneaux, and the Poggio a'Frati Riserva sees some new oak. IGT Toscanas include the international varieties and focus on monovarietals: Le Pratolo is Merlot, Buriano is Cabernet Sauvignon, and Molino delle Balze is Chardonnay. The Stielle IGT was a blend of Sangiovese and Cabernet Sauvignon, from a single vineyard, but became a monovarietal Sangiovese in 2007. "We used to need something stronger to support the Sangiovese, but with our new clone, we don't need that support," says winemaker Rolando Bernacchini. "The drive here is that the market is looking for single varieties and we didn't have a 100% Sangiovese super Tuscan, so we decided to make Stielle 100%," he explains. Stielle was relabeled as a Gran Selezione Chianti Classico when the category was created. The 2 ha of Cabernet Sauvignon in the Stielle vineyard are now added to the 4 ha plot for Il Buriano. The village of Castagnoli is a charming environment in which to taste these wines. The Riserva gives a more serious impression than the Chianti Classico *tout court*, and makes a modern impression. Il Buriano is firm but fresh—"The freshness is the characteristic of the terroir," says Rolando—and ages well.

Rocca di Montegrossi *

ROCCA DI MONTEGROSSI
San Marcellino
Chianti Classico

Fraz. Monti In Chianti, 53010 Gaiole in Chianti (SI)

(39) 0577 747977

Marco Ricasoli-Firidolfi

roccadimontegrossi@chianticlassico.com

www.roccadimontegrossi.it

Chianti Classico

San Marcellino, Gran Selezione

Chianti Classico Vin Santo

20 ha; 100,000 bottles

[map p. 43]

This old estate was established in the eighth century and has continued by descent to Marco Ricasoli-Firidolfi. Located on a high point in Monti in Chianti, looking out over the valley from 350m elevation, today its 100 ha include equal areas of vineyards and olive groves. (The thousand olive trees are almost all the Coreggiolo cultivar, so the olive oil can be considered a monovarietal). The wine has been produced on the estate since Marco restored the buildings in 1999 (previously it was made at another family property).

There are two Chianti Classicos, both including indigenous varieties as well as Sangiovese; the estate wine has Canaiolo and Colorino, and is about half of all production, while Vigneto San Marcellino, now labeled as a Gran Selezione, is produced only in top vintages, and includes some Pugnitello. The IGT Toscana Geremia is a blend of two thirds Merlot to one third Cabernet Sauvignon. The estate Chianti Classico ages in botti for a year and a half, while San Marcellino and Geremia age in a mixture of barriques and tonneaux, including about half new wood, for two and a half years. San Marcellino is much richer than the Chianti Classico, showing the concentration of old vines and its exposure to barriques; it is somewhat reminiscent of Brunello. Geremia shows the Italian take on the Bordeaux blend, with Cabernet structure in the background behind the soft richness of Merlot. There's a split in style between the freshness that balances the fruits of the Chianti Classico, and the richness of the Gran Selezione and the super-Tuscan. The Vin Santo comes from late harvest grapes that are dried on moveable racks in a modern loft, is highly botrytized, and ages for seven years in very small casks of a wood mix of oak, cherry, and mulberry; it's very rich.

Ruffino

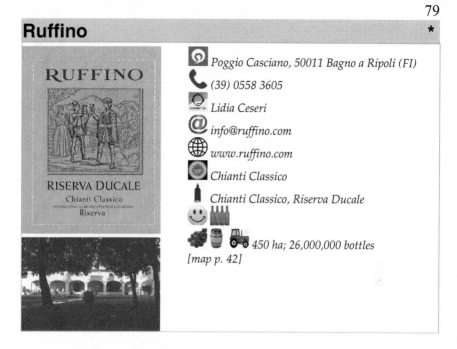

RUFFINO

RISERVA DUCALE
Chianti Classico
Riserva

Poggio Casciano, 50011 Bagno a Ripoli (FI)

(39) 0558 3605

Lidia Ceseri

info@ruffino.com

www.ruffino.com

Chianti Classico

Chianti Classico, Riserva Ducale

450 ha; 26,000,000 bottles

[map p. 42]

Owned by conglomerate Constellation, Ruffino is one of the largest producers in Chianti. Founded in 1877 as a small producer by the Ruffino cousins, who were traders in wine, Ruffino started in Chianti, and then grew in the second half of the twentieth century by purchasing further estates in Montalcino and Montepulciano as well as Chianti. The Folonari family, who owned Ruffino since 1913, sold a 40% share to Constellation (who had been handling distribution) in 2004, and then in 2011 Constellation took complete ownership. The estate vineyards still belong to the family, but are rented to Constellation on 25-year contracts; they provide about a third of all grapes. The original winery at Pontassieve, close to Florence, is now used for administration and bottling.

The estates under the Ruffino umbrella include four in the Chianti area: Montemasso, Poggio Casciano, Santedame and Gretole. In addition, there are Greppone Mazzi (in Montalcino), La Solatia (near Siena, which produces white wine), and Lodola Nuova (in Montepulciano). Poggio Casciano sits on the border between Chianti Classico and Chianti Ruffina. Gracious old buildings are set behind a park, with the family residence at one side, surrounded by vineyards; it's the hospitality center for Ruffino. The estates, however, are not always emphasized as the wines are identified by the Ruffino brand. Outside of Chianti Classico, subregions are not used, and the wine is just identified as Chianti. In Chianti Classico, grapes may come from more than one estate.

The style of the Chianti Classicos shows a viscous sheen to the palate, perhaps helped by the common inclusion of Merlot. Santedame could be a Riserva but is not labeled as such in order to emphasize its origins; it's soft and smooth. The flagship Chianti Classicos are the Riserva Ducale and the Riserva Ducale Oro, now a Gran Selezione. These are modern blends of 80% Sangiovese with Cabernet Sauvignon and Merlot, the first coming from Gretole, Santedame, and Montemasso, and the Oro from Gretole and Santedame. With production of more than a million bottles, brand consistency is important for Riserva Ducale, which is aged in Slavonian casks. The Ducale Oro, which comes only from estate grapes, and is aged in barriques followed by casks, shows a more structured character. Made only in best vintages since 1947 as a selection from Riserva Ducale, it has a surprising capacity to age: the 1977 was still lively in 2016. The elegant style of the Brunello shows greater purity and precision than the Chianti Classicos. Some of the DOCG wines and super-Tuscans are identified with specific estates, with the Colorino-Merlot blend Romitorio di Santedame coming from the estate. From Poggio Casciano, Modus has more or less equal proportions of Sangiovese, Merlot, and Cabernet Sauvignon, and is a mainstream super-Tuscan, if there is such a thing, while the newest cuvée, Alauda, is a blend of Merlot, Cabernet Franc, and Colorino, and makes a more forceful international impression. There's also a range of white and sparkling wines.

Agricola San Felice *

IL GRIGIO
da San Felice

SAN FELICE
AGRICOLA

📍 Loc San Felice, 53019 Castelnuovo Berardenga *(SI)*

📞 *(39) 0577 39 91*

👤 *Roberta Martini*

@ *info@agricolasanfelice.it*

🌐 *www.agricolasanfelice.it*

Chianti Classico

🍷 *Il Grigio, Gran Selezione*

🏭! 🏭 ⊗

🍇 🚜 *216 ha; 1,270,000 bottles*

[map p. 43]

Located at the southern border of Chianti Classico, San Felice was owned by the Grisaldi Del Taja family, who were influential in establishing the appellation. In 1968, the estate was sold to the industrial group Aesculapius, who put a well known Sangiovese expert, Enzo Morganti, in charge. In 1978, the estate was purchased by an insurance group in Milan which subsequently became part of Allianz Group, a financial conglomerate. The vineyards at San Felice are in a 360 degree circle around the village. The estate was expanded first by buying two more properties in Chianti Classico in 1981, Villa Pagliaia and San Vito, and then by buying the Campogiovanni estate in Montalcino in 1982.

San Felice has been associated with a significant research program, as Enzo Morganti established an experimental vineyard, known at San Felice as the Vitarium, where clones of Sangiovese were developed; then this was extended into research on Tuscany's other indigenous varieties. The 2 ha vineyard now has 200 grape varieties. One consequence has been the reintroduction of Pugnitello, which is now a significant proportion of some of the estates.

The Chianti Classico is Sangiovese with 10% each of Pugnitello and Colorino; "we look for drinkability more than power, so aging is one year in Slavonian casks," says marketing manager Fabrizio Nencioni. The Il Grigio Riserva and Gran Selezione are blends of 80% Sangiovese with five indigenous varieties; The Riserva ages in a mixture of Slavonian casks and

French tonneaux (none new), while the Gran Selezione is all tonneaux (one third new). I like the savory sense of the garrigue that comes from the combination of Sangiovese and indigenous varieties.

Poggio Rosso is a single vineyard where Enzo Morganti planted selected clones of Sangiovese and Colorino, from which a single vineyard wine was produced; some Pugnitello has been included since 2004. Pugnitello has become something of a specialty: "we performed microvinifications, we liked the results, so in 1997 we planted 12 ha, and it's now the second most important variety here," says Fabrizio. A monovarietal Pugnitello has been produced since the 2003.

The super-Tuscan Vigorello has changed its character many times, from 100% Sangiovese in 1968, to a Bordeaux blend in 2006. "It was very good but we felt it was lacking Tuscan typicity," so since 2011 it has been a blend of Pugnitello with the Bordeaux varieties. "The addition of the Pugnitello obviously changed the style a lot," says Fabrizio. There are really two threads here. Chianti Classico and Il Grigio Riserva follow the route of lively fresh red fruits, while Poggio Rosso, Pugnitello, and Vigorello show a more opulent, spicy black fruit style. The estate is well into oeno-tourism as the most recent development was the conversion of the entire hamlet at San Felice into a hotel.

Tenuta Tignanello ***

⊙ *Via Santa Maria a Macerata, 50026 San Casciano in Val di Pesa (FI)*

📞 *(39) 0552 35 95*

Stefano Carpeto

@ *antinori@antinori.it*

🌐 *www.antinori.it/en/26-generazioni/wines/estates/3*

Chianti Classico

🍾 *IGT Toscana, Tignanello*

🚜 *90 ha; 500,000 bottles*
[map p. 42]

"In 1966, Antinori bought Cabernet Sauvignon from France and planted it at Tignanello together with Sangiovese. At the time other producers were quite hostile," recollects winemaker Stefano Carpeto. Tignanello actually started as a Chianti in 1970, labeled as Chianti Classico riserva vigneto Tignanello, with a more or less conventional blend of Sangiovese with Canaiolo, Trebbiano, and Malvasia, although it defied convention by aging in French barriques, rather than casks of Slavonian oak. The next vintage it became a Vino da Tavola della Toscana and was just called Tignanello. The white grapes were dropped from the blend, and the Cabernet was introduced. Since 1982 its constitution has been 85% Sangiovese, 15% Cabernet Sauvignon, and 5% Cabernet Franc (depending on the vintage).

Under the present rules it could be reclassified to Chianti Classico, but "Tignanello has too much quality to be a Chianti Classico," says Stefano. However, "It's a super-Tuscan but you can feel the soul of Chianti," says Sara Pontemolesi, winemaker at Antinori's Chianti Classico winery close by. Indeed, winemaker Renzo Cotarella says, " I have my idea of the super-Tuscans. I think a wine should be considered a super-Tuscan if it is a Sangiovese blend because Sangiovese is the representative of Tuscany. That's why I consider Tignanello to be the *real* super-Tuscan."

Another super-Tuscan, Solaia, comes from the same estate, from vineyards adjacent to those for Tignanello. Solaia's first vintages in 1978 and 1979 were 80% Cabernet Sauvignon and 20% Cabernet Franc, but since then it has essentially been the inverse of Tignanello, with 80% Cabernet Sauvignon to 20% Sangiovese. "This is our top wine," says Sara Ponte-molesi. Personally, I find the savory character of Tignanello more intriguing. (There's a story that Solaia started by accident, because there was too much Cabernet to be used for Tignanello in 1978.) Solaia ages in 100% new oak, whereas Tignanello has 50% new oak.

The Antinori Marchese Chianti Classico Riserva now also comes from the Tignanello estate (before 2011 it also included other sources), and as a similar blend to Tignanello is sometimes regarded as a mini-Tignanello. However, it is not a second wine; although grapes could in theory be declassified from Tignanello, this does not happen. The vineyards at Tignanello are at an elevation of 200-400m, and the terroir is based on albaresa; in fact, the vineyards now have a white appearance, as the stones were brought up to the surface during replanting and pulverized to create a reflective layer. The elevation helps to explain the taut quality of the wines. For me, Tignanello is a quintessential modern Tuscan wine, with a savory palate reflecting the character of Sangiovese, and the structure brought by Cabernet Sauvignon never overwhelming it.

Castello Vicchiomaggio   *

⦿ *Loc. Le Bolle, via Vicchiomaggio, 4, 50022
Greve in Chianti (FI)*

📞 *(39) 0558 54079*

Federica Matta

@ *info@vicchiomaggio.it*

🌐 *www.vicchiomaggio.it*

Chianti Classico

La Prima, Gran Selezione

Chianti Classico Riserva, Agostino Petri

🙂 🏭 ✖

35 ha; 400,000 bottles
[map p. 42]

Almost at the northern limit of Chianti Classico, the Castello is a historic monument. There's been a castle on the site since the eleventh century; the main building is a Renaissance villa dating from the fifteenth century, but the tower, which contains the aging cellar, dates from about 1100. Today the buildings house the winery, a hotel (with an additional building given over to apartments), and a restaurant (occupying a gracious room in the villa). There's a wine shop and tasting room just off the main road at the start of the access road that winds up through the south-facing vineyards, rising from 300m to the castle at 500m. The shop offers a wide range of wines, olive oils, and other products.

"Our family has always been in wine and spirits. It was my grandfather who really created the winemaking business here. He was in spirits, in London, and bought Vicchiomaggio when he retired in 1964. My father started making wine here in 1975," says Federica Matta. The estate of 120 ha has 35 ha of vineyards and 10 ha of olive trees. The estate was in poor condition, but a steady replanting program and other investments saw the wines begin to gain a reputation in the eighties. There is also a 15 ha property in Maremma, Villa Vallemaggiore; grapes are crushed there, and the juice is transported to Vicchiomaggio for aging.

Vicchiomaggio produces three Chianti Classicos and two super-Tuscans. All are blends of Sangiovese with international varieties, except for the most recent IGT Toscana. Chianti Classico San Jacopo has 5% Cabernet Sauvignon, which increases to 10% in the Riserva Agostino Petri (named for an owner in the early twentieth century). Chianti Classico matures for 8 months in botti: "We like to be on the new vintage very soon, we like to have it fruity and crisp," says Federica. The Riserva spends 18 months in a mix of botti and barriques, and the Gran Selezione, which comes from a 2 ha plot, and has 10% Merlot, ages in new barriques for 24 months.

Going from Chianti Classico to Riserva, the tart, fresh quality becomes smoother and rounder, and the fruits become more black; the trend intensifies going to the Gran Selezione, which is more powerful, but all the wines show that touch of savory character, with a hint of gunflint, that is characteristic of Sangiovese. All the wines are blends: Chianti Classico has 5% Cabernet Sauvignon, which increases to 10% in the Riserva. The Gran Selezione has 10% Merlot. The international varieties no doubt contribute to the relatively dark color, but are subservient to Sangiovese in the aroma and flavor profiles. The IGT Toscana Ripa Della More moves in a more international direction, with an equal blend of Sangiovese to international varieties (Cabernet and Merlot), but Sangiovese remains dominant albeit with some spice giving a more modern impression. The 100% Merlot of FSM, which comes from a 4 ha plot where the soil is clay-based, shows softness on the palate, but the wine still has the characteristic freshness of Tuscany.

Fattoria di Viticcio *

Via San Cresci 12/a, Greve in Chianti (FI)

(39) 0558 54210

Beatrice Landini

info@fattoriaviticcio.com

www.fattoriaviticcio.com

Chianti Classico

Chianti Classico Riserva, Beatrice

50 ha; 250,000 bottles

[map p. 42]

Viticcio has extended from its origins in Chianti in 1964 to vineyards in Bolgheri and Maremma. Viticcio at Greve in Chianti remains the main estate, devoted mostly to the production of Chianti Classico, although there are 10 ha of Cabernet Sauvignon for the Monile super-Tuscan blend with Merlot, introduced in 1998. At the other extreme, Bere is an IGT Toscana blend from all the young vines. The Chianti Classico is Sangiovese with 2% Merlot, the Riserva has 5% Merlot and 5% Syrah, and Beatrice Gran Selezione has 5% Cabernet Sauvignon. Prunaia is a 100% Sangiovese, originally an IGT Toscana, but now a Chianti Classico Gran Selezione. All are aged in a mixture of Slavonian oak casks and barriques. Under the name of Tenuta I Greppi, the 15 ha vineyard in Bolgheri produces the Greppicaia Bordeaux blend, and its second wine, Greppicante. The only white wine is the small production of Greppico from Vermentino at Maremma. The wines are quite modern in style, and perfectly well made, but for me do not really exhibit the typicity of Tuscany. Supposedly it's possible to make an appointment to see the winery, but you are more likely to get a brief tasting in the tasting room.

Castello Di Volpaia **

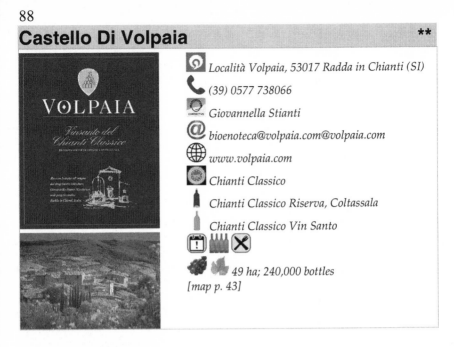

VOLPAIA
Vinsanto del Chianti Classico

📍 *Località Volpaia, 53017 Radda in Chianti (SI)*

📞 *(39) 0577 738066*

Giovannella Stianti

@ *bioenoteca@volpaia.com@volpaia.com*

🌐 *www.volpaia.com*

⬤ *Chianti Classico*

🍷 *Chianti Classico Riserva, Coltassala*

🍷 *Chianti Classico Vin Santo*

📅 🏭 ✖

🍇 🍷 *49 ha; 240,000 bottles*

[map p. 43]

Visiting Volpaia is a completely different experience from the usual winery. There is no single winery, but facilities are spread around various buildings in the mountaintop hamlet of Volpaia, a fortified medieval village. In addition to the buildings that house the winery equipment, there's a hotel, restaurant, and wine shop. One building has fermentation tanks, there are a couple with barrel cellars, there is one with a bottling line—the facilities are spread all around the hamlet. A piping system hidden below the streets moves the wine from upper levels to lower levels by gravity. "This is not a commercial approach, we will never make money in wine, so our philosophy is that we should at least do something we like," says Giovanna Stianti. Volpaia is unique, we are working in an old place where wine was made two centuries ago; it is absolutely mad. If we had any idea of what would happen, we would never have done this.

Giovannella's father originally bought Volpaia as a hunting reserve, but the government subsequently cancelled all hunting rights, and subsequently gave the gave the estate to Giovannella and her husband, Carlo Mascheroni. The Castello di Volpaia owns about two thirds of the village, which is given over to the winery and associated activities. The road up to the hamlet winds through the vineyards of the 360 ha estate, rising from 450m to 650m. All except one of the vineyards are on this hill, facing south or southwest. The single vineyard wines come from plots at the higher elevations. "The soil is very particular," Giovannella says, "no one has the same soil, so the wines are very distinctive, you may like them or not."

Well, I do like them. The relatively sandy soils are reflected in the lightness and elegance of the wines. The Chianti Classico is 90% Sangiovese and 10% Merlot. "The Sangiovese is very good, but it needs three years; the Merlot makes the wine approachable a bit sooner," Giovannella says. The three single vineyard wines are produced most years, but not every year. Because it did not include white grapes, Coltassala was originally labeled as a vino da Tavola in 1980, but after the change of rules in 1998 it became a Chianti Classico Riserva (it has 95% Sangiovese and 5% Mammolo). Il Puro is a monovarietal Sangiovese, and comes from the Casanova vineyard, on the south-facing slope between the Coltassala and Balifico vineyards. It comes from 25 cultivars of Sangiovese that were propagated from very old vines. Produced in very small amounts, the first vintage was 2006, and it became a Gran Selezione, although "it's more a project than a Gran Selezione." Balifico is the IGT Toscana, with 35% of Cabernet Sauvignon and 65% Sangiovese.

The same style runs through all the wines, smooth and silky. Going from Chianti to the Crus, there is more of that bite of Sangiovese. Coltalassa Riserva balances between minerality and more chocolaty notes, and the Il Puro Gran Selezione shows deep concentration. The IGT Toscana, Balifico, moves in a rounder more international direction within the same house style. These are extremely elegant wines. There are also monovarietal wines, Vermentino and Cabernet Sauvignon, from an estate purchased in Maremma in 2007.

Brunello di Montalcino

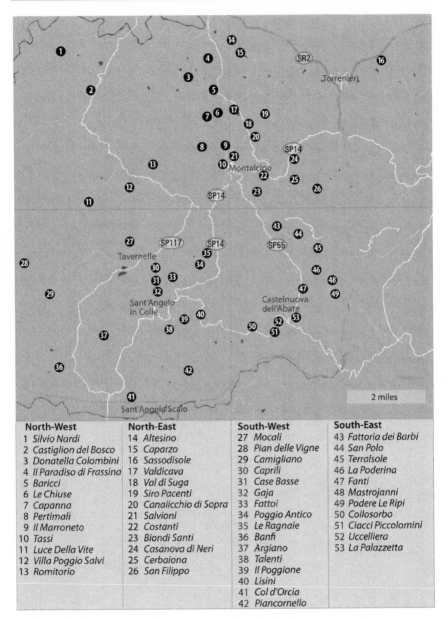

2 miles

North-West	North-East	South-West	South-East
1 Silvio Nardi	14 Altesino	27 Mocali	43 Fattoria dei Barbi
2 Castiglion del Bosco	15 Caparzo	28 Pian delle Vigne	44 San Polo
3 Donatella Colombini	16 Sassodisole	29 Camigliano	45 Terralsole
4 Il Paradiso di Frassina	17 Valdicava	30 Caprili	46 La Poderina
5 Baricci	18 Val di Suga	31 Case Basse	47 Fanti
6 Le Chiuse	19 Siro Pacenti	32 Gaja	48 Mastrojanni
7 Capanna	20 Canalicchio di Sopra	33 Fattoi	49 Podere Le Ripi
8 Pertimali	21 Salvioni	34 Poggio Antico	50 Collosorbo
9 Il Marroneto	22 Costanti	35 Le Ragnaie	51 Ciacci Piccolomini
10 Tassi	23 Biondi Santi	36 Banfi	52 Uccelliera
11 Luce Della Vite	24 Casanova di Neri	37 Argiano	53 La Palazzetta
12 Villa Poggio Salvi	25 Cerbaiona	38 Talenti	
13 Romitorio	26 San Filippo	39 Il Poggione	
		40 Lisini	
		41 Col d'Orcia	
		42 Piancornello	

Altesino

***

Brunello di Montalcino
Denominazione di Origine Controllata e Garantita
Imbottigliato nelle cantine di Palazzo Altesi
da Altesino SpA, Montalcino - Italia

Vendemmia

0,750 litri   PRODOTTO IN ITALIA   13,5% vol.

Località Altesino 54, 53024 Montalcino (SI)

(39) 05778 06208

Simone Giunti

info@altesino.it

www.altesino.it

Brunello Di Montalcino

Brunello Di Montalcino

47 ha; 220,000 bottles

[map p. 90]

Altesino is the northernmost producer in Montalcino, right at the boundary of the commune. It was owned by the Consonno family before being sold to Elisabetta Angelini, owner of the adjacent Caparzo property, in 2002. Altesino and Caparzo had been one property before 1970, but remain separate today. "Altesino is more masculine, it's on the north side of the hill, the weather is colder," Elisabetta says. Three vineyards totaling about 25 ha are close to the winery, and another vineyard of 15 ha is south of Montalcino. The famous Montosoli vineyard of 7 ha is on a hill a couple of miles from the winery.

Altesino have the traditional belief that the best wine is made by blending the richer, firmer wines of the south with the more elegant wines of the north, with the exception of course of the Montosoli single vineyard bottling. Montosoli has long been regarded as special for the power of its wines, and Altesino were among the first to introduce the Cru concept into Montalcino when they started to make a separate cuvée in 1975. Altesino source all their vines from Montosoli by selection massale, but even so get different results in different locations, so they believe the special quality of Montosoli derives more from the terroir than the clone. Aside from Montosoli, the Riserva comes from the very best grapes, while the Rosso mostly comes from young vines.

Large casks of Slavonian oak are used to age the Rosso and the Brunello; barriques are used for the IGT (including Palazzo Altesi, which is 100% Sangiovese but is labeled as IGT to distinguish it from the Brunello and Rosso); and about 10% of Montosoli spends 3-4 months in barriques. (In this context, Altesino's reputation for having introduced barriques into Montalcino is a bit misleading; it is true, but it was not for the Brunello.) At one point, Altesino had four IGTs, but the number has been steadily reduced to focus more on the appellation. Palazzo Altesi has smoothness from oak aging, the Rosso is smooth and approachable, but shares with the Brunello a deceptive structure that is hidden in the background by the fine texture of the palate. Montosoli has an extra density in its black fruits and that hidden structure ensures long aging. The Riserva has more evident structure behind its chocolaty tannins. The overall impression is quite modern.

Argiano ★★

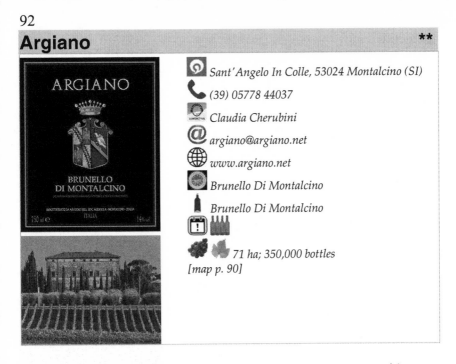

Sant'Angelo In Colle, 53024 Montalcino (SI)

(39) 05778 44037

Claudia Cherubini

argiano@argiano.net

www.argiano.net

Brunello Di Montalcino

Brunello Di Montalcino

71 ha; 350,000 bottles

[map p. 90]

One of the founding members of the Consorzio, Argiano is an old estate, but now undergoing a transition resulting from changes in ownership. Dating from the sixteenth century—the original villa from 1598 is still standing—it was owned by the Cinzano spirits company before it passed to Noemi Cinzano in 1992 after Cinzano was sold to a drinks conglomerate. Introducing French oak, she followed a generally modernist style, with the famous oenologist Giacomo Tachis as her consultant. About half of the vineyards are classified for Brunello, and another 7 ha of the youngest vines are dedicated to Rosso. It's located in the southwest, and Argiano sees itself as representing the warmer part of Montalcino.

Argiano was sold in 2013 to a group of Brazilian investors, who have put resources into replanting the vineyards and renovating the winery. Following a soil survey, vineyards are being changed, a new aging cellar was built in 2015, and a new vinification cellar is planned. "They are returning to tradition, using concrete vats for fermentation and MLF, and as of the 2015 vintage there won't be any use of French oak (in Brunello)," says Claudia Cherubini at Argiano. (Previously vinification in stainless steel was followed by aging in one year barriques and Slavonian botti for the Rosso, and in a mixture of barriques and tonneaux for the Brunello.)

The IGT Suolo, a monovarietal Sangiovese from the oldest vineyards, aged exclusively in new French barriques, has been discontinued. "The focus is on Brunello, they don't want to make an IGT from Sangiovese any more." A more conventional super-Tuscan, Solengo, with half Cabernet

Sauvignon, and equal proportions of Petit Verdot, Merlot and Syrah, continues to be aged in new barriques of French oak. Introduced by Tachis, the intention was to show how powerful and long lived it could be. The most recent cuvée was the IGT NC (Non Confunditur), a blend of Cabernet Sauvignon, Merlot, Syrah, and Sangiovese, intended to be easy to drink and directed at the market in the United States; it is now almost half of all production. Argiano is definitely moving from the camp of the modernists towards tradition for its Brunello, with the IGTs remaining more international in style.

Banfi   *

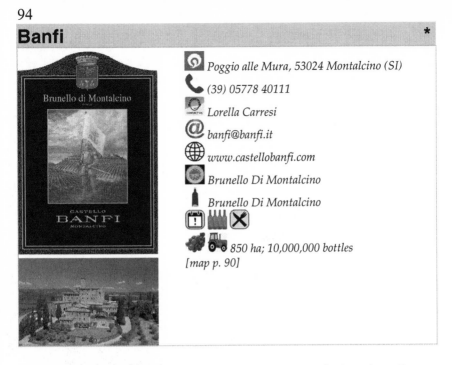

Poggio alle Mura, 53024 Montalcino (SI)

(39) 05778 40111

Lorella Carresi

banfi@banfi.it

www.castellobanfi.com

Brunello Di Montalcino

Brunello Di Montalcino

850 ha; 10,000,000 bottles

[map p. 90]

Banfi Wines was founded as an American importer of wines from Europe in 1919 by John Mariani and is run today by his grandchildren. Castello Banfi in Montalcino was founded in 1978 as the first wine producer in the company, expanded with the purchase of vineyards in Chianti Classico, Bolgheri, and Maremma. Castello Banfi remains the heart of the company, located in a complex of old buildings at the southern border of Montalcino, in the former hamlet of Poggio alle Mura, which also includes a hotel and restaurant.

The extensive vineyards were planted through a land-clearing program that involved removing several hills. Around the complex, six lakes have been constructed for irrigation (of IGT wines). Banfi is the largest producer in Montalcino, although somewhat controversial locally because a major part of its plantings started with international varieties. The winery is full of modern equipment, including tanks specially designed for Banfi which are stainless steel at top and bottom, but wood in between, designed because they believe fermentation in wood gives better results, but poses hygiene problems. Winemaker Lorella Caresi says that the tanks "give wine with better aromatics and color, although science does not explain the difference between wood and steel."

Banfi started by producing wines under all the DOCs of the region (Brunello and Rosso di Montalcino and Sant'Animo), but then moved away from Sant'Animo to the IGT Toscana—"no one knows Sant'Animo."

So Summus (a blend of Sangiovese, Cabernet Sauvignon, and Syrah), Excelsus (a Merlot-Cabernet Sauvignon blend) are now super-Tuscans. These and the newer super-Tuscan cuvées are aged in barrels. The Rosso and Brunello di Montalcino age in a mixture of different wood sizes; the smallest barrels are usually 350 liters.

With about 30% new oak on average, there tends to be a noticeable oak component to the super-Tuscans, and the Brunellos are quite powerful, often needing time for tannins to resolve. The single vineyard wines, identified as Poggio alle Mura, come from the oldest vineyards, immediately by the castle (planted in 1984) and age mostly in barrels. There are both Rosso and Brunello from the Poggia alle Muro vineyard, and the structure is more evident than in the communal wines. The Poggio all'Oro super-cuvée, made only in top years, ages in only barrels. There is an impression locally that the wines are intended to appeal to the American palate.

Fattoria Dei Barbi

★★

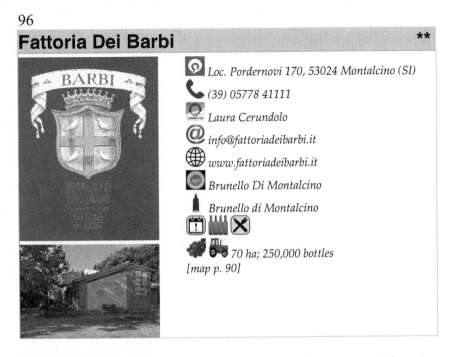

◎ Loc. Pordernovi 170, 53024 Montalcino (SI)

☎ (39) 05778 41111

◎ Laura Cerundolo

@ info@fattoriadeibarbi.it

⊕ www.fattoriadeibarbi.it

◉ Brunello Di Montalcino

🍾 Brunello di Montalcino

🔲 ♨ ✖

🍇 🚜 70 ha; 250,000 bottles

[map p. 90]

"We have more or less lived the history of Montalcino," says Stefano Colombini, whose family came to the area in 1352. Initially they built a castle at Poggia alle Mura (now part of the Banfi estate), and they acquired the Barbi estate by marriage in 1790. The family also own estates in Chianti, and they purchased an estate in Maremma in 1997. The vineyards of the estate in Montalcino are mostly near the winery, but there are also rented vineyards elsewhere.

Barbi is firmly in the camp of traditional producers. "I believe in tradition, I believe we have to work in the spirit of tradition, but we need to use modern methods. So we have been pioneers for using dry ice for fermentation, we use the most modern stainless steel fermenters. We follow a mixture of the best traditions and the best techniques to produce Brunello that must be as similar to tradition as possible." Aging is mostly in large botti, but this is not rigid, with smaller casks used for smaller plots. And there's a distinction based on conditions. "We use smaller vats for wines that have more tannins. For lighter vintages we use larger vats."

Five wines come from the estate in Montalcino. Brusco dei Barbi, labeled as IGT Toscana, is a second wine from Sangiovese plus small amounts of indigenous varieties. Rosso di Montalcino comes from younger vines, and the Brunello is the major wine, about 40% of production; its blue label is one of the best known in Montalcino. The top two wines are made only in the best vintages: the Riserva is made by selection from the estate, and Vigna del Fiore is a selection from a single (5.7 ha) vineyard in the southern part of the appellation. Compared with the 200,000 bottles of Brunello, there are only 10,000 bottles of Riserva and 4,000 bottles of Vigna del Fiore.

The Rosso and Brunello show the same smooth style, with finely textured tannins, but the Brunello has more depth and flavor variety. The Riserva is more complex and structured. Vigna del Fiore shows greater silkiness on the palate, with more refinement rather than power. Stefano's objective is to make wines that can be drunk on release but that age well, and accordingly the Brunello 2011 was already ready to drink in 2016, but the Vigna Del Fiore needed another couple of years. The wines age for decades: a tasting at the winery showed the 2007 just beginning to develop, the 1986 still going strong, and the 1982 fully developed—after 35 years! Barbi is unusual in keeping back enough wines from each vintage that they can still offer quite old vintages for sale

Biondi Santi ***

Via Pier, 1, 53024 Montalcino (SI)

(39) 05778 48087

Jacopo Biondi Santi

biondisanti@biondisanti.it

www.biondisanti.it

Brunello Di Montalcino

Brunello Di Montalcino

26 ha; 60,000 bottles

[map p. 90]

This is really the grandfather estate for all Brunello since the appellation was more or less created by Biondi Santi in the nineteenth century. Ferruccio Biondi-Santi was instrumental in planting a strain of Sangiovese which he called Brunello (little brown one) at a time when most plantings were white. From phylloxera through the first part of the twentieth century, his son Tancredi Biondi-Santi was one of the few to continue producing Brunello. The estate was managed by Tancredi's son Franco from 1970, and by Franco's son Jacopo since 2013.

The tradition of selecting cultivars has continued with a project started in 1970 which culminated in development of clone BBS/11 (Brunello Biondi Santi), which is now used for replanting. The heart of the estate is the Greppo vineyard and winery just south of Montalcino (but sometimes a little difficult to find; people with morning appointments have been known to turn up in the afternoon...) Vineyards face east, with elevations up to 500m. There are also vineyards at Pieri (close to Il Greppo), and north of Montalcino, allowing Biondi-Santi to follow the traditional model of blending wines from the south and north. In fact, this is probably the most traditional producer in Montalcino; accordingly, the wines can be unbending when young, and require years to age. Cuvées are distinguished by age of vines.

The White Label Rosso di Montalcino comes from vines less than ten years old, the Fascia Rosso comes from older vines from lots that are declassified in the lesser vintages (the entire crop was declassified in 2002), the Annata Brunello comes from vines of 10-25 years age, and the Riserva comes from vines over 25 years only in top vintages. Needless to say, vinification is entirely traditional: after fermentation in cement tanks, the wine is transferred to Slavonian botti for aging. The wines tend to elegance rather than power, with that faintly savage quality of Sangiovese in the background, and the Brunello beginning to come around after a decade, the Riserva just a little longer. They remain the archetypal Sangiovese. Biondi-Santi is committed to Sangiovese even to the extent of making a 100% Sangiovese from a separate estate, the Castello di Montepo, in Maremma, but this is a quite different expression of the variety, softer and denser, and more southern.

Given the history in Montalcino, It was a shock when it was announced at the end of 2016 that a majority stake had been sold to the owners of Charles Heidsieck and Piper Heidsieck Champagne, although Jacopo continues to make the wine.

Castello di Camigliano *

Via d'ingresso 2, 53024 Montalcino (SI)

(39) 0577 844068

Sergio Cantini

info@camigliano.it

www.camigliano.it

Brunello Di Montalcino

Brunello di Montalcino

92 ha; 350,000 bottles

[map p. 90]

When you arrive in the hamlet of Camigliano, the only sign of the winery is a shop and tasting room just below the village. The offices for the winery are in one of the houses just off the little square that is the center of the village. The old winery, and a new extension, are built unobtrusively into the hillside just beside the village (total population: 25). The estate of 500 ha is all around the village, at an elevation about 300m. It was acquired in 1957 by entrepreneur Walter Ghezzi, and today is run by his son Gualtiero.

Camigliano is a traditional producer. "We use large wood casks, I prefer big barrels, especially when the grapes are perfect, and I don't like to smell vanilla or wood in the wine. I don't like too much extract, which makes the first glass taste good, but not the second," says winemaker Sergio Cantini. Brunello is about half of total production, and the Rosso is about a quarter.

Camigliano is in the south of Montalcino, but the wine style is fresh. A white comes from a 2 ha plot of Vermentino and is quite lively. The entry-level red is an IGT Toscana, Poderuccia, a Merlot-Cabernet blend, with a little Sangiovese, intended for immediate consumption. A Chianti Colli Senesi comes from a negociant activity. The Rosso di Montalcino is distinct from the Brunello. "For us it is important the Rosso should be fresh and drinkable."

The Brunello makes a savory impression, quite fresh and crisp; the Gualto Riserva is more structured. A single vineyard wine, Paessagia Inatteso (which means unexpected landscape) was introduced with the 2012 vintage (the next vintage will probably be 2015). It is matured in 25 hl barrels (compared with 60 hl for Brunello), and moves more towards black fruits. Whereas the Brunello is ready five years after the vintage, Paessagia Inatteso is more structured and requires longer. The wines are a solid representation of the traditional style.

Canalicchio di Sopra ***

Loc. Casaccia, 53024 Montalcino (SI)

(39) 05778 48316

Francesco Ripaccioli

info@canalicchiodisopra.com

www.canalicchiodisopra.com

Brunello Di Montalcino

Brunello di Montalcino

20 ha; 70,000 bottles

[map p. 90]

"Our wines are an expression of the blend between Canalicchio and Montosoli," says winemaker Francesco Ripaccioli, who runs this estate together with his brother Marco (who manages the vineyards) and sister Simonetta. The estate was founded by Primo Pacenti in 1962 and became one of the founding members of the Consorzio, Primo's son-in-law, Pier Luigi Ripaccioli joined in 1987, and now it is in the hands of the third generation. The property is just off the main road going north from Montalcino, and although it looks entirely modern, there's a huge excavation for building a new underground cellar. It is focused entirely on Brunello.

The original vineyards are in Canalicchio—just on the other side of the road from the winery is the original house together with a hotel—and the vineyards on Montosoli came into the family in 1985. An extra 2 ha were planted in 2014 and another 2 ha were purchased in 2015; "it wasn't the right moment, " says Francesco, "because we are building a new cellar and this is a very big investment, but the plot was in the middle of our vineyards so we decided to buy." Presently 70% of the vineyards are in Canalicchio and 30% on Montosoli hill. "We are one of the few producers to have vineyards only in the north. The two zones of production are very close but very different. Our wine represents the north side of Montalcino but it also represents our style; the minerality comes from Montosoli and the richness comes from Canalicchio."

The major distinction between cuvées is age of the vines, with vines of 3-10 years age used for Rosso, 10-25 years for Brunello, and the oldest vines for the Riserva (in the best vintages only). The Rosso ages in an equal mix of French tonneaux and Slavonian botti, the Brunello only in Slavonian botti, and the Riserva uses tonneaux followed by botti. The Rosso shows a fine balance between red fruits and minerality, the Brunello is more powerful and complex, more black fruits than red, but retains that characteristic balance with minerality although showing more vintage variation—"we like to make different wines depending on the vintage," says Francesco—and the Riserva (made only 15 times since 1970) shows the rich side of Brunello, but matures in the elegant house style. For me, the Brunello is the perfect compromise.

Although the Ripacciolis believe in blending, the current project is to introduce a single vineyard wine with the 2015 vintage. This is Vigna Casaccia—"this is the most elegant vineyard we have, not the best, but the most elegant." Barrel samples promise a wine with the richness of the vintage but the elegance of the house style. I believe that right across the range, these were the most elegant wines I tasted on my most recent visit to Montalcino.

Caparzo **

Strada Prov Del Brunello Km 1, 70, 53024 Montalcino (SI)

(39) 0577 848390

Massimo Bracalente

caparzo@caparzo.com

www.caparzo.com

Brunello Di Montalcino

Rosso di Montalcino, La Caduta

90 ha; 90,000 bottles
[map p. 90]

Caparzo was founded in 1970, just after the establishment of the Consorzio in Brunello. By the nineties, after several changes of ownership, it was somewhat in decline, until it was purchased by Elisabetta Gnudi Angelini in 1998, when vineyards were replanted and the winery was modernized. Elisabetta also owns Borgo Scopeto in Chianti Classico, and DOGA delle Clavule in Maremma. After Caparzo, she subsequently bought the adjacent Altesino property, but "Caparzo is on the south side of the hill, it's more feminine, but very strong," she says.

The estate covers 200 hectares, with nine separated vineyards in several different areas of the appellation devoted to Brunello. The most famous is La Casa, a 5 ha vineyard on the hill of Montosoli with galestro terroir, which has been the basis of a single vineyard wine since 1977. Production is poised between modernism and tradition. The "classic" Rosso, Brunello, and Riserva are blends from vineyards in both the north and south, and are aged only in large casks, but the two single vineyard wines, Brunello La Casa and Rosso La Caduta use tonneaux of French oak. The Riserva comes from La Casa, La Caduta, and Il Cassero. Rosso La Caduta is an unusual Rosso, coming from a single vineyard, a plot of 7.5 ha in the south of the appellation; the explanation is that "the winemaker really wanted to do it." The super-Tuscan, Cà del Pazzo is a blend of Sangiovese and Cabernet Sauvignon, aged only in tonneaux, and there is also a dry white wine, Le Grance, that ages in small barrels.

The style is rich and firm, more modern than traditional, and going from the Rosso La Caduta or Brunello to the Riserva and La Casa, the wines become denser and more chocolaty; overall the style is more modern than traditional.

Caprili

**

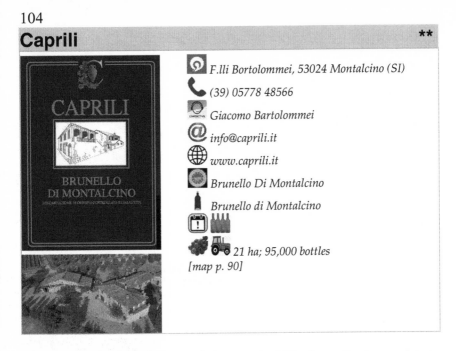

F.lli Bortolommei, 53024 Montalcino (SI)

(39) 05778 48566

Giacomo Bartolommei

info@caprili.it

www.caprili.it

Brunello Di Montalcino

Brunello di Montalcino

21 ha; 95,000 bottles

[map p. 90]

The Bartolommei family were tenants on the Villa Santa Restituta estate in the southwest quadrant of Montalcino, until they purchased the Caprili property in 1965. "They were making wine, but it was just table wine," says Giacomo Bartolommei. The estate has 60 ha, including 18 ha of Sangiovese, 3 ha of white grape varieties, and 4 ha of olive trees. Vineyards are maintained by an equal mix of selection massale from the original vineyard, and a clone Giacomo found in Chianti. "We want a clone where the berries are not too large and the bunches are not too compact," Giacomo explains. The new winery, completed in 2015, and built on two levels into the hillside, sits in the middle of what feels like a broad plateau extending to mountains in the distance.

The first Brunello dates from the 1978 vintage, and since 1983 the Riserva has been made from the oldest vines (dating from 1955) in the best vintages, thirteen times to date. It essentially comes from one 3,000 liter cask. The Rosso comes from the youngest vines. "We consider ourselves a traditionalist in using large casks for aging. Just in the past few years we've started to use some smaller sizes (700 liter)," says Giacomo. Wood is mostly Slavonian oak, with a little French. The style shows a classic progression from the light, attractive palate of the Rosso to the refined palate of the Brunello, where fruits make a precise impression on the palate. Purity of the fruits of Sangiovese drives the palate, which is traditional in prizing elegance over power. The IGTs include a red from Sangiovese and a white from Vermentino; there's also a Sant'Antimo white as a "hobby wine," which is aged in barrique, and a sweet Moscadello.

Casanova di Neri   *

Pod. *Casanova, 53024 Montalcino (SI)*

(39) 05778 34455

Giacomo Neri

info@casanovadineri.com

www.casanovadineri.com

Brunello Di Montalcino

Brunello di Montalcino, Cerretalto

65 ha; 220,000 bottles
[map p. 90]

"We believe our vineyards give us the possibility to produce three different expressions of Montalcino," says Giacomo Neri. Giacomo's father bought the estate in 1971, and it has remained a family property. A modern winery operating by gravity feed on three levels was built into the hillside in 2005, just beside the house where the tasting room and offices are located. The vineyards are located in several areas, some around the winery in the northeast, some farther east, and some to the south at Sant'Angelo.

The entry level wines are IGT Toscana, one white and one red. The Rosso comes from dedicated vineyards. "To us it's the first wine of our hierarchy, not a second wine," says Giacomo, who regards the IGT as the second label (the red is a blend of Sangiovese with Colorino). I find the Rosso easy going. The Brunello, known as the white label, comes from three vineyards in the northeast; aged in botti, it gives more structured impression, but remains generally soft. Then there are three single vineyard wines, or perhaps more accurately, three single terroir wines.

Coming from the most recently acquired vineyards, Figurante represents two vineyards, one the highest of the estate in the northeast, the other on a plateau in the east. Tenuta Nuova comes from two very similar vineyards at high elevation in the south, where conditions are dry, and represents the more opulent side of Montalcino. Cerretalto comes from the oldest vineyard, close to the winery, at one of the coolest locations in Montalcino (it ripens three weeks after Nuova): it has by far the most structured impression. Made only in the best vintages, and aged in small barrels for an extra year, it could be a Riserva, but "Cerretalto is Cerretalto," Giacomo says.

Made since 2000, the super-Tuscan monovarietal Cabernet Sauvignon, Pietradonice, comes from a vineyard in the south, and even after a decade's aging conveys a powerful impression of warm climates; "this is a Montalcino version of Cabernet," according to Giacomo. The style here ranges from the quaffable IGT or Rosso, to more solid Brunello, and expressions of terroirs ranging from mineral to opulent.

Case Basse Di Soldera ***

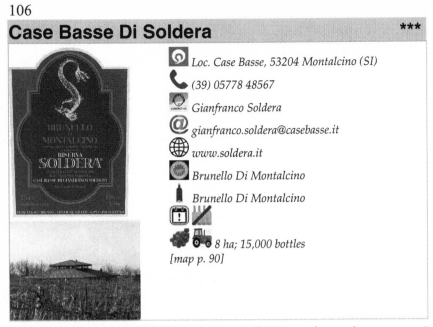

Loc. *Case Basse, 53204 Montalcino (SI)*

(39) 05778 48567

Gianfranco Soldera

gianfranco.soldera@casebasse.it

www.soldera.it

Brunello Di Montalcino

Brunello Di Montalcino

8 ha; 15,000 bottles

[map p. 90]

"My wine, like all the finest wine in the world, is simply not for everyone," says Gianfranco Soldera, which gives a pretty good impression of the prickly personality behind what were formerly some of the best wines of Brunello di Montalcino. "Formerly," because after a disagreement with the Consorzio, Gianfranco resigned, and then was expelled just to make sure; so now the wines are labeled as IGT Toscana.

It can be difficult to track the identity of the individual cuvées. When Gianfranco, then an insurance broker, bought the estate in 1972, the land had been more or less abandoned, and he planted two vineyards, Case Basse and Intistieti, about 400m apart, more or less at the same elevation of 320m. The Brunello used to come sometimes from Case Basse, sometimes from a blend of the two vineyards. Riservas might come from either or both. At one period there was a Vino da Tavola labeled Intistieti, but actually coming from both vineyards; this was effectively a second wine. The current IGT Toscana is a blend from both vineyards.

Gianfranco is one of the most vociferous advocates for keeping Brunello as 100% Sangiovese, so it is not surprising that winemaking is traditional: the underground cellar was constructed using only natural materials (stone and iron), grapes are destemmed and go into vats of Slavonian oak, and the temperature of fermentation (by indigenous yeast only, of course) is not controlled; malolactic fermentation usually starts immediately the alcoholic fermentation has finished, and then the wine ages for four or five years in Slavonian botti. Gianfranco has strong views on barriques: "they are for deficient wines that don't get enough tannins and flavor from the grapes." The wine is held in the cellar before release; the 2009 was the most recent vintage on the market in 2016. Intended to be the definitive description of Sangiovese, the wines are among the most expensive coming from Montalcino.

Castiglion del Bosco *

Località Castiglion del Bosco, 53024 Montalcino (SI)

(39) 05778 07078

Anna Malvezzi

wine@castigliondelbosco.com

wine.castigliondelbosco.com

Brunello Di Montalcino

Brunello di Montalcino, Campo del Drago

62 ha; 250,000 bottles

[map p. 90]

The hamlet of Castiglion del Bosco used to be a commune focused on producing honey and wine. Today the hamlet has been turned into a hotel; the spa is where the communal winery used to be. After Massimo Ferragamo purchased Castiglion del Bosco in 2003, a new gravity-feed winery was built just along the road. Ferragamo's ownership shows in the professional arrangements for hospitality: most visitors come from the hotel. There is a wine club (with its own room in the winery), and there are events and dinners.

There are two separate vineyards. Just to the south, the main vineyard of 42 ha, south-facing at 420m elevation with classic galestro soils, produces Brunello. Just east of the hotel, on slightly lower ground with more clay, a 20 ha vineyard produces Rosso di Montalcino. A single vineyard wine, Campo del Drago, comes from a 1 ha plot at the northeast corner of the main vineyard: this is the highest elevation, with the best exposure. The Riserva comes from eight hectares just near it.

The style has been changing towards a more traditional approach, but is still more modernist than traditionalist. "The market makes it sensible for us to produce wine that people can drink immediately," says Communication Manager Anna Malvezzi. Aging regimes differ with the cuvée. "Before Ferragamo came in 2003, there was a very French style here, with lots of barriques. Now we are trying to go back to tradition and we are buying larger casks for aging." The Brunello ages for one year in small casks and one year in large casks. Campo del Drago spends two years in barriques. The Riserva spends three years in large casks.

Intended for immediate consumption, the Rosso is fresh and lively. The Brunello adds some weight, but the overall impression remains fresh.

Campo del Drago shows greater refinement, with a smooth roundness reflecting its time in barriques. The Riserva shows a greater sense of power and an increased sense of concentration. The overall impression remains relatively modern.

Massimo also has a winery on the Tuscan coast, Prima Pietra, north of Bolgheri, making a Bordeaux blend. There are plans to introduce a limited edition all-Cabernet blend of 85% Cabernet Sauvignon to 15% Cabernet Franc. The wines were made at Castiglion del Bosco until 2017, when a new cellar was built at Prima Pietra.

Cerbaiona ★★★

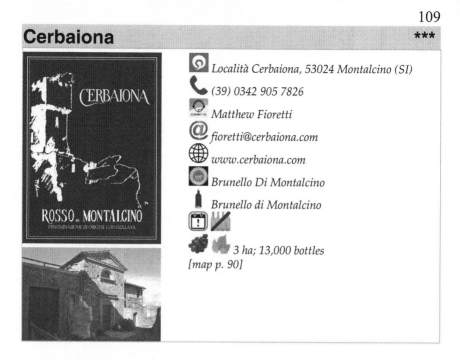

Località Cerbaiona, 53024 Montalcino (SI)

(39) 0342 905 7826

Matthew Fioretti

fioretti@cerbaiona.com

www.cerbaiona.com

Brunello Di Montalcino

Brunello di Montalcino

3 ha; 13,000 bottles

[map p. 90]

"This destination is not on the digital map," my GPS announced, when I entered the coordinates for Cerbaiona, but we knew the destination was in sight when we saw the huge crane looming over the construction. The buildings are in full flight of reconstruction with a two year project to renovate and extend the cellars, improve the vineyards, and plant a new vineyard. Cerbaiona is one of the mythic producers of Brunello, created when Diego Molinari left Alitalia in 1977, and instead of flying planes, began making wine. Winemaking might more accurately have been called idiosyncratic rather than traditional, with vinification in cement tanks with fiber glass lining, and aging in very old botti. But the wines won world-wide acclaim.

Cerbaiona was a manor house, and the east-facing vineyards just below the house are adjacent to the La Cerbaiola estate. Cerbaiona was purchased in 2015 by a group of investors led by Matthew Fioretti, a Californian who spent some of his education in Italy, and started in wine by importing Italian wines into the United States. Now he is living at Cerbaiona and managing the massive reconstruction. "I thought we could do it one step at time, but I realized we would have to do everything at once," Matthew explains. Just below the house a 1 ha olive grove has been re-planted with vines, and an additional vineyard may be added at slightly higher elevation (the estate is at 450 m).

"The Molinaris were the ultimate garagistes, making some wine in the basement," is how Matthew describes the previous situation. Working around the construction, the current vintage is being made in new equipment, with wood fermenters and new botti. So there may be a bit more wood showing for the next year or so. Tastings of the Rosso and Brunello presently maturing in botti show the characteristic combination of density with elegance. Will there be any permanent change in style? "Well, it's the vineyards that count," Matthew says, but there will be better handling of the fruit, so look for increased purity in the wine.

Ciacci Piccolomini d'Aragona *

○ *Località Molinello, 53024 Castelnuovo Dell'abate, Montalcino (SI)*

☎ *(39) 05778 35616*

○ *Alessandra Avanzati*

@ *marketing@ciaccipiccolomini.com*

⊕ *www.ciaccipiccolomini.com*

◉ *Brunello Di Montalcino*

▮ *Brunello di Montalcino, Pianrosso*

▮ *Sant'Antimo, Fabius*

☺ ▥

🍇🚜 *56 ha; 300,000 bottles*

[map p. 90]

The unusual name of the winery reflects the conjunction of two families, Ciacci and Picolimini d'Aragona, which started as an arranged marriage in 1921. In 1985, the Countess died without progeny and left the estate to the winemaker, Giuseppe Bianchini. He designed and built the new facility in 2003. His children Paulo and Lucia took over in 2004.

The estate of 220 ha is on the unpaved road that connects Saint Angelo to Castelnuova dell'Abate. In addition to 54 ha of vines, it has 40 ha of olive trees. A new winery was built into the hillside in 2003; previously the wine was made in the Palazzo (acquired from the Church by the family in the nineteenth century) in the village of Castelnuova dell'Abate. A wine shop and tasting room were built on the other side of the road in 2013.

"We are absolutely a traditional producer," says Alessandra Avanzati. "Everything is aged in 60-75 hl botti of Slavonian oak. We think the Slavonian oak is less aggressive, softer, than French or American oak. We are looking for the elegance of Sangiovese rather than the power of oak." The Rosso ages for a few months, a second Rosso, called Rossofonte, for a year, Brunello for 36 months, and Riserva for 42 months.

The estate produces two Rosso di Montalcino, and three Brunellos in top vintages. The classic Rosso is typically soft and approachable and comes from dedicated vineyards. Produced in much smaller amounts, Rossofonte is declassified from Brunello, and is more restrained, intense, and structured, but still shows the juiciness of Rosso. It bears much the same relationship to the classic Rosso as the Riserva does to the regular Brunello. Most of the vineyards are at 250-350m, but the Riserva and single vineyard wine, Pianrosso, come from 7 plots at 180m, totaling 12 ha, that are just above the river Orcia, in a warm area that has the oldest vines. Pianrosso is the most sophisticated of the Brunello cuvées, smooth and silky, with precise mineral impressions. The Brunellos make a more modern impression than might be expected from the traditional production methods.

The estate produces two wines under the Sant'Antimo DOC from international varieties, aged in barriques. Ateo's name is a joke, meaning atheist (as opposed to Sangiovese's meaning of God). It started in 1989 as a blend of Cabernet Sauvignon, Merlot, and Sangiovese, but the Sangiovese was removed in 2007, and since then it has been a Bordeaux blend. Although it has equal proportions of Cabernet and Merlot, it shows more the plushness of Merlot than austerity of Cabernet. Fabius is a monovarietal Syrah that has been made from a 2 ha plot since 1996: its style follows the Northern Rhône, and it has the lowest alcohol of any of the Ciacci wines. There is also an entry-level IGT Toscana based on Sangiovese plus some international varieties. In addition, Ciacci owns the Santo Stefano in Grosseto which produces a Montecucco Sangiovese.

Col d'Orcia ★★

BRUNELLO
DI MONTALCINO

COL D'ORCIA

📍 Via Giuncheti, Sant'Angelo In Colle, 53024 Montalcino (SI)

📞 (39) 05778 0891

Count Francesco Marone Cinzano

@ info@coldorcia.it

🌐 www.coldorcia.it

Brunello Di Montalcino

Brunello Di Montalcino Riserva, Poggio al Vento

142 ha; 800,000 bottles

[map p. 90]

Located on the Sant'Angelo hill, this is a beautiful property with vineyards all around the winery at the end of a long unpaved road. Col d'Orcia is one of the larger producers in Montalcino, but still retains the feel of a small family winery. Vineyards are planted with 18 clones that were developed on the property. The approach to viticulture and winemaking is traditional, looking for subtlety rather than extraction. "We pick each vineyard three to four times," says Francesco Cinzano, "not necessarily waiting for the highest ripeness at each picking; some are picked to preserve acidity, some are picked to get high sugar levels. Our intention is to get a good blend of acidity, sugar, and phenolics in the wine."

Maturation is in traditional casks of Slavonian oak for the regular Brunello and Riserva. The Brunello ages for 36 months as in the old protocol; and the Riserva age for 48 months. As the result of experimentation with alternative aging methods, there is now a Nastagio cuvée of Brunello which is aged in tonneaux. The top wine is the single vineyard Poggio al Vento Riserva, which comes from a single plot in the center of the estate. Rosso comes partly from dedicated vineyards, partly from younger vines, but has now been divided into the Rosso *tout court* (the entry level wine) and the Banditella Rosso, which is selected from a single vineyard and fills a gap between Rosso and Brunello.

The house style is smooth and elegant in a modern mode, and shows all along the range. There is increased precision and a finer sense of structure moving from Rosso to Brunello to Riserva. Francesco believes you get the best results for Sangiovese by reducing oxidative exposure, so barriques are used only for international varieties. These are labeled under the Sant'Animo DOC: Olmaia is a monovarietal Cabernet Sauvignon, and Nearco is a blend of Cabernet, Merlot, and Syrah. There's also a Chianti and some Pinot Grigio.

Donatella Cinelli Colombini

⊙ *Loc Casato, 53024 Montalcino (SI)*

📞 *(39) 05778 49421*

Antonella Marconi

@ *vino@cinellicolombini.it*

🌐 *www.cinellicolombini.it*

◉ *Brunello Di Montalcino*

🔺 *Brunello di Montalcino Riserva*

😊 🍺

🍇 🍇 *17 ha; 90,000 bottles*

[map p. 90]

This is a relatively new estate as an independent venture, but a very old one in terms of the history of the family and the region. The Colombini family owned Barbi (in the southeast of Montalcino), Casato Prime Donne (in the northwest of Montalcino), and Fattoria del Colle (in the Orcia region to the northeast of Montalcino). "The estate was inherited from my grandmother to my mother, who divided it in 1998," explains Donatella, who now runs both Casato Prime Donne and Fattoria del Colle. At Casato Prime Donne she produces Rosso and Brunello di Montalcino (before 1998 the grapes went into Barbi, which is now a separate estate); at Fattoria del Colle she produces IGT Toscana and Orcia (based on blends of Sangiovese with other varieties). Casato Prime Donne and Fattoria del Colle each has roughly the same area of vineyards. The same team, consisting exclusively of women, makes the wine at both.

The estate is in a single parcel, located on a very long unpaved road, but can be quite busy when coach parties arrive at the tasting room. The winery is behind the old buildings. "This was all in disrepair, I had to rebuild it," Donatella says. There are four wines: Rosso and Brunello each account for about 45% of production; Selection Prime Donna and Riserva are about 5% each. Lots are assigned to Rosso on the basis of ripeness—"when you taste, it is obvious which should be Rosso and which should be Brunello," Donatella says. "Prime Donna is a selection from a plot where the quality is better every vintage, but no one has explained the basis for the difference."

"We are a traditionalist: wines are aged in botti. The innovation here is a return to the past; in the Middle Ages, vats were small and open, so that's what we use here," she says. "The open tops mean the wine gets oxygenation during fermentation, and we get a better balance." Quantities for

Selection Prime Donna and the Riserva are small, so the wines are fermented in concrete eggs rather than vats. The Brunello ages in tonneaux for a year and then for another year in Slavonian foudres. Selection and the Riserva age for longer in botti, and go back in the concrete eggs for six months before bottling.

The Rosso is immediately approachable with a hint of structure at the end. The Brunello is a little deeper, and a classic representation of Sangiovese, tending towards a savory flavor spectrum, the Riserva is riper and if anything more approachable, and Prime Donna moves in a more chocolaty direction. Going from Brunello to Riserva to Prime Donne, the wines become more finely textured and silkier, more elegant rather than more powerful. I would be inclined to describe the style as moving from more traditional towards more modern along the series.

Lisini

Sant'Angelo In Colle, Loc. Casanova Lisini 53024 Montalcino (SI)

(39) 0577 864040

Carlo Lisini Baldi

azienda@lisini.com

www.lisini.com

Brunello Di Montalcino

Brunello Di Montalcino

24 ha; 90,000 bottles

[map p. 90]

One of the oldest estates in Montalcino, the property has been in the family since the mid nineteenth century, and was one of the founding members of the Brunello Consorzio in 1967. Today it's run by third generation cousins Lorenzo, Carlo, and Ludovica. The estate covers 154 ha, of which only a small part is planted to vineyards. The oldest plantings of the modern era date from the 1930s, although within the estate there's an isolated half hectare vineyard with pre-phylloxera vines dating from the mid-nineteenth century, and for more than twenty years from 1985 this was bottled as the separate prefillossero cuvée, until production from the vineyard became too low.

The vineyards are exclusively devoted to Sangiovese, planted with clones that were developed on the estate. Vinification is traditional, with fermentation in glass-lined or stainless steel tanks followed by maturation in Slavonian botti, briefly for the Rosso, longer for Brunello and the Riserva, which comes from a selection of the best lots. There is also a single vineyard wine, Ugolaia, from a 1.5 ha vineyard high up in the estate. The IGT San Biagio is effectively a second wine that is aged only in stainless steel. The style is pure Sangiovese, with a savory palate showing some savage hints, a classic representation of the unsullied variety.

Luce Della Vite

**

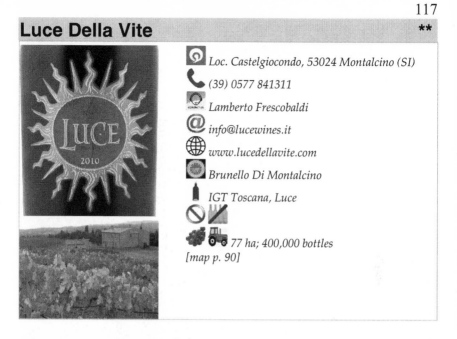

⊙ *Loc. Castelgiocondo, 53024 Montalcino (SI)*

📞 *(39) 0577 841311*

Lamberto Frescobaldi

@ *info@lucewines.it*

🌐 *www.lucedellavite.com*

Brunello Di Montalcino

🍾 *IGT Toscana, Luce*

🚫 ⚒

🍇 🚜 *77 ha; 400,000 bottles*

[map p. 90]

Adjacent to Castelgiocondo, which is Frescobaldi's estate in Montalcino, Luce della Vite started in 1995 as a joint project between Frescobaldi and Robert Mondavi of Napa Valley. It became Frescobaldi's alone after Mondavi was sold to Constellation. The focus is really on a super-Tuscan blend of Sangiovese and Merlot, not on Brunello. The first two vintages of Luce, 1993 and 1994, the super-Tuscan, were released together in 1997. Lucente is a second wine, from the same vineyards, and has been made since the 1995 vintage. There are generally up to 100,000 bottles of Luce and 300,000 of Lucente. The Brunello comes from a specific 5 hectares on the estate and has been made since 2003; its production is small compared with the super-Tuscans, only about 20,000 bottles.

Mastrojanni

Podere Loreto San Pio, 53024 Castelnuovo dell'Abate, Montalcino (SI)

(39) 05778 35681

info@mastrojanni.com

www.mastrojanni.com

Brunello Di Montalcino

Brunello di Montalcino

33 ha; 110,000 bottles
[map p. 90]

The estate was created in 1975 by Gabriele Mastrojanni, a lawyer who lived in Rome. By the 1990s it was managed by his son, Antonio, but after Gabriele died in 2008, it was sold to the Illy family (of coffee fame). Francesco Illy had purchased the neighboring property, Podere Le Ripi, in 1997, so when Mastrojanni became available, he was instrumental in the Illy group's decision to purchase it. Andrea Machetti arrived as winemaker in 1992, and still is involved today. The new winery, a practical modern building on the track from Castelnuova dell'Abate to Sant'Antimo, was constructed in 2011. The vineyards are all around, at an elevation of 420m. There's also accommodation at the Mastrojanni Relais.

"We consider ourselves a traditional producer," they say. Fermentation takes place in concrete vats because "we believe that stainless steel damages the wine." The wines age in relatively small botti (16-40 hl) of Allier oak. There are no barriques: "we don't want toast and oak in our wines." There are four wines from Montalcino. The Rosso di Montalcino is declassified from Brunello, there is just a little less of the Brunello than Rosso, and there are two single vineyard wines, Vigna Schiena d'Asino and Vigna Loreto, produced in only 300-400 cases each. There is no Riserva—"we prefer to focus on the single vineyards"—so all the Brunellos spend the same 36 months in wood. In addition, San Pio is a blend of 20% Sangiovese with 80% Cabernet Sauvignon, which spends 18 months in tonneaux, and is now labeled as IGT Toscana instead of Sant'Antimo as previously.

The style is quite sleek and elegant. The Rosso gives a good preview of the style of the Brunello, which is rounder and deeper. The Sant'Antimo follows the same general style, but has less persistence. Notwithstanding the exclusive focus on botti, the elegant style seems poised somewhere between full fledged tradition and modernist.

Siro Pacenti   ***

Podere Pelagrilli, 53024 Montalcino (SI)

(39) 0577 848662

Giancarlo Pacenti

info@siropacenti.it

www.siropacenti.it

Brunello Di Montalcino

Brunello di Montalcino

Brunello di Montalcino

24 ha; 60,000 bottles

[map p. 90]

This estate is generally considered an arch modernist, but it has always been one of my favorites because the style is never overdone and the purity of fruits shines out. Before 1970 the Pacentis were farmers rather than wine producers; they owned the property, but it was given over to polyculture. Siro started producing wine in 1970, but the current style and reputation date from his son Giancarlo's return from Bordeaux, where he studied oenology.

When Giancarlo came back he wanted to follow the French philosophy, but with traditional grapes. He received a lot of criticism at the beginning, when he introduced selection in the field, a sorting table, and French oak. Rosso and Brunello are aged only in barriques; the Riserva ages in tonneaux. All cuvées receive the same mix of new and old oak, with about one third new. A new cellar was built in 2008; Giancarlo wanted to represent his style— he likes modernity—and it's very stylish in an ultramodern fashion.

The estate is focused entirely on Brunello. There are vineyards around the cellar in the northern part of the appellation, and some more about 25 km away in the southern area. There are no dedicated vineyards for Rosso; the Rosso is about half of production, but comes entirely from declassification. "Our Rosso has the same character as Brunello, sometimes people call it a baby Brunello. But there was no choice between Rosso and Brunello, we wanted to have something more approachable, but with the character of Brunello." This led to the introduction of Pellagrilli in 2006.

The main distinction between the three cuvées is the age of the vines: less than 15 years for Rosso, 15-25 years for Pellagrilli, more than 30 years for Brunello. The Riserva comes from a specific 2 ha vineyard, half of which has vines planted by Siro in 1967. With the exception of the Riserva, all cuvées are blends in the traditional way from vineyards in both north and south. The style is consistent across the range: the Rosso is a baby Brunello with some wild edges, Pellagrilli is smoother but lighter than the Brunello, which is rich and chocolaty, and displays the full style of the house. Sweetness and concentration of fruits increase going up the scale.

La Palazzetta

Podere La Palazzetta , Castelnuovo Dell'Abate, 53024 Montalcino (SI)

(39) 05778 35631

Luca Fanti

palazzettafanti@gmail.com

www.palazzettafanti.it

Brunello Di Montalcino

Brunello di Montalcino

20 ha; 70,000 bottles

[map p. 90]

This is very much a family business, now making its transition to the next generation, Luca Fanti and his sister Tea. "My parents (Flavio and Carla) started in 1980 with animals and cereals," Tea says, "with only 1 ha." The first Brunello was produced in 1988: now there is also a Rosso and a Riserva. A Sant'Antimo Rosso has been made since 1999.

Just outside Castelnuova dell'Abate, the winery is on a high point overlooking the village, off the track that leads to Sant'Antimo. A small cluster of buildings house a fermentation cellar with stainless steel vats, an aging cellar crammed with botti, and a small bottling line. It's very hands on: Flavio established the style of a firmly traditionalist producer, his wife Carla designed the labels, Luca is now the winemaker, and Tea is in charge of marketing.

"We only have indigenous grapes, you won't find any international varieties here," Tea explains. In fact, the only variety aside from Sangiovese is Colorino. "Grandfather had some Colorino, which he used for governo (using partially dried grapes to help with fermentation), but now it's blended with Sangiovese in the Sant'Antimo." Brunello ages in old 40 hl botti of oak from Allier, now circular rather than the original ovals, "to preserve the fruit better." The Rosso and Sant'Antimo age in tonneaux (500 liter casks), because the wine is not intended for long aging; a little new oak is used for the first three months.

The style is firmly traditional, but is moving towards greater approachability. When I arrived, Luca was engaged in a blending session with consulting oenologist Maurizio Saettini. "The wine should be ready to drink almost as soon as it goes on the market," Maurizio says "The wines have been very good, but used to need a lot of time. We are working to make them rounder, but they should also last."

There are five separate vineyards. The oldest vineyards tend to be used for Brunello, vineyards of 10-20 years age for Rosso di Montalcino, and the youngest vineyards for Sant'Antimo, but all are treated the same. "Everything is picked as though for Brunello," says Tea, "the lots that are more fruity and fresh are used for the Rosso to give a more forward style." The Riserva comes from a specific plot of calcareous terroir in the best years. They may be committed to a traditional style, but there is some innovation. In 2016, Luca produced a rosé as an experiment, and the Sant'Antimo is bottled using a new type of cork produced from sugar cane.

The same style runs through the range, but shows greater depth and refinement moving along the hierarchy. The rosé, all Sangiovese, is quite full. Sant'Antimo actually contains several indigenous varieties, "planted all together in the ancient style." It's forward and fruity, and attractive for enjoying immediately. The Rosso di Montalcino is a little darker, with more of a sheen. The Brunello is a smoother version of the Rosso, more restrained and less obvious, with a very fine structure. Rosso and Brunello both show a touch of salinity at the end—"this is something you find in all our wines," Luca says.

Sassetti Livio Pertimali ***

Str. Consorziale dei Canali, 329, 53024 Montalcino (SI)

(39) 0577 1698316

Sabina Sassetti

info@pertimalisassetti.it

www.pertimalisassetti.it

Brunello Di Montalcino

Brunello Di Montalcino

16 ha; 50,000 bottles

[map p. 90]

The Sassettis have been making wine in Sant'Angelo for three generations, but Pertimali is a relatively recent creation, dating from the 1970s when Livio Sassetti sold the property in Sant'Angelo and bought the Pertimali property on a hill in the northwest part of Montalcino. About 10 ha surround the vineyard, with another 2 ha in the south. "Blending between the vineyards from north and south is important for producing high quality wine," Livio says. There are no vineyards dedicated to Rosso, which is produced exclusively from declassified Brunello, and is vinified exclusively in steel. The amount of Rosso varies widely, depending on the vintage; in 2002 it was the whole crop.

The Brunello and Riserva (made only in top vintages) are produced traditionally, with aging in Slavonian botti. The super-Tuscan Fili di Seta is a blend of 60% Sangiovese to 40% Cabernet Sauvignon; originally it was equal proportions of each variety, "but the Cabernet overwhelmed the Sauvignon," Livio explains. The Sassettis bought an estate in Maremma in 2000 and make wine under the Montecucco DOC. "The attraction is that you can buy land and convert it to vineyards; it is not affordable to buy more vineyards in Montalcino," Livio says. The wines have a classic flavor profile, showing the savory side of Sangiovese; and Fil di Seta shows Sangiovese more clearly than Cabernet. The style conveys an impression of refinement.

Pian Delle Vigne ★★

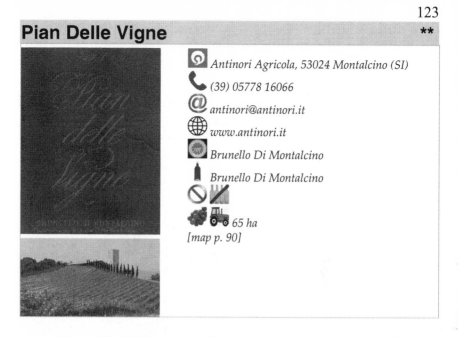

Antinori Agricola, 53024 Montalcino (SI)

(39) 05778 16066

antinori@antinori.it

www.antinori.it

Brunello Di Montalcino

Brunello Di Montalcino

65 ha

[map p. 90]

Just to the south of Montalcino, Pian delle Vigne takes its name from an old railroad station located on the property. Antinori bought the property in 1995. Most of the estate is planted to vines. Brunello has always been produced, but the Rosso di Montalcino was introduced only in 2014. The Rosso is smooth and elegant, but perhaps more in line with the top Chianti Classicos than the Brunello, which can be rich (reflecting the southern location of the vineyards in Montalcino) or more restrained, depending on the year. Although the style seems modern, the Brunello is aged in large (80 hl) casks. The Riserva, Vigna Ferrovia, made only in best vintages, ages first in tonneaux and then is transferred to 30 hl casks. These are extremely reliable wines.

Gaja (Pieve Santa Restituta) **

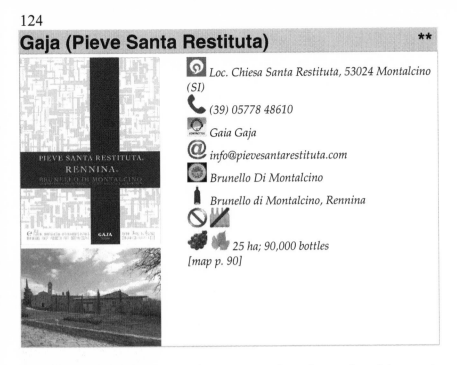

⊙ Loc. Chiesa Santa Restituta, 53024 Montalcino (SI)

📞 (39) 05778 48610

Gaia Gaja

@ info@pievesantarestituta.com

Brunello Di Montalcino

🍾 Brunello di Montalcino, Rennina

🚫 🏭

🍇 🍂 25 ha; 90,000 bottles

[map p. 90]

Pieva Santa Restituta is one of those estates where the quality of the terroir shines out from the wines. The property belonged to the local diocese until 1972 until it was sold (including the church) The wines were good, but improved after Gaja bought the property in 1994. At first they continued to be labeled under the Pieve Santa Restituta name, but in due course this was replaced by Gaja's striking black and white labels.

There was a large-scale restructuring of the vineyards between 2005 and 2010, but the same two cuvées continue to be made: Rennina, which is a blend of three parcels with sandy soils; and Sugarille, which comes from a single parcel with more calcareous soils. Rennina tends to be more savory, Sugarille denser and more chocolaty. In addition, there is a Brunello *tout court*, which comes from a 9 ha vineyard Gaja purchased in 2007 in the north of Montalcino. A new underground winery was constructed in 2005.

Vinification isn't determinedly either modern or traditional as the Brunellos are all fermented in stainless steel and then have same aging regime of a year in barriques (first to third year) followed by a year in botti. The style of the wines seems to have become more obviously modern in the past decade, but remains in the direction of elegance rather than power, showcasing purity of fresh black fruits.

Poggio Antico   **

Loc. *Poggio Antico, 53024 Montalcino (SI)*

(39) 05778 48044

mail@poggioantico.com

www.poggioantico.com

Brunello Di Montalcino

Brunello di Montalcino

33 ha; 90,000 bottles

[map p. 90]

"We are a modernist producer, but we want to accommodate all tastes, this is why we produce two different styles of Brunello," says Paola Gloder. Located just to the south of Montalcino within an estate of 200 ha, mostly forested, Poggio Antico is one of the highest wineries in the appellation, sitting on top of a hill at 450m. The estate was created in 1984 when Giancarlo and Nuccia Gloder came to Montalcino from Milan; today it is managed by their daughter Paola. The buildings were renovated in 2002, and the winery is underground. Vineyards are all around the winery—"all are within five minutes of the sorting table," they like to say. All 30 ha of Sangiovese are declared for Brunello (although some goes into the super-Tuscans), and there are also 2 ha of Cabernet Sauvignon and 1 ha of Petit Verdot. The Rosso is exclusively declassified from Brunello; it ages in French tonneaux, but has a light style.

It's impossible to define a single style, because there are two extremes. The traditional Brunello ages in Slavonian botti and conveys a savory impression with mineral notes. Altero comes from the same vineyard, but is aged for two years in new French tonneaux and makes a much riper, richer impression. (Originally it was an IGT, because when it was introduced in 1983 the rules required more than two years' aging for Brunello) The Riserva comes from the oldest vines and spends a year in new tonneau followed by two years in Slavonian oak, but the overall impression is much closer to Altero than to the traditional Brunello. I find the traditional Brunello to be the most elegant, and it ages beautifully, reaching a peak of delicacy after more than a decade. The super-Tuscans, Madre (equal blend of Sangiovese and Cabernet Sauvignon), and Lemartine (50% Sangiovese and 25% each of Cabernet Sauvignon and Petit Verdot) are powerful wines in the international style.

All the wines except the Rosso and the "traditional" Brunello are well into modernism, and I'd give Poggio Antico one star as a modernist but two stars as a traditionalist. There is an excellent restaurant at the winery, where it's possible to have dinner after a tour and tasting.

Villa Poggio Salvi ✱

POGGIO
SALVI
DI
Montalcino

📍 *Loc. Poggio Salvi, 53024 Montalcino (SI)*

📞 *(39) 05778 47121*

👤 *Luca Belingardi*

@ *vps@villapoggiosalvi.it*

🌐 *www.villapoggiosalvi.it*

🔵 *Brunello Di Montalcino*

🍾 *Brunello di Montalcino*

🚜 *42 ha; 200,000 bottles*

[map p. 90]

"The estate was created in 1979 by my grandfather, who came from Milan and bought a country house with a couple of hectares of vineyards. There wasn't any intention to make wine, but little by little the estate enlarged and now there are 20 ha in a single block around the winery. They are on galestro soils at 350-500m elevation. In 1998, he bought another 20 ha in Chianti Colli Senesi," says Luca Belingardi, who has been at the winery since 2008, and took charge in 2012. Driving into the estate, you pass a group of imposing buildings that include the residence, and then you come to the purpose-built concrete winery, buried in the hillside. Grapes from all the vineyards are vinified here.

Two wines come from the vineyards in Chianti. Just over half the vineyards make Chianti Colli Senesi; the minor part is IGT Toscana. The grape mix is similar, Sangiovese with 10-15% Merlot, but the Chianti ages only in steel and is more overtly fruity and fresh, while the IGT Toscana has six months in oak, and is a little smoother. "Considering that we have Rosso di Montalcino, we like the Chianti Colli Senesi to be easy and approachable," Luca says.

On the local estate, the Rosso comes mostly from younger vines, but may include some declassified Brunello, and continues theme of showing direct fruits. Moving to the Brunello, there is a jump in intensity and more of a savory edge. In addition to the general Brunello, there are two special cuvées; both Pomona and the Riserva come from specific 1 ha plots. All the wines are aged in botti. "We don't use barriques, only big botti of Slavonian oak, 60-110 hl. We think Sangiovese ages better in the botti," Luca says. Rosso ages for 12 months, Brunello and Pomona for 30 months, and the Riserva for 36 months. Moving from the general Brunello to the special cuvées, there is more flavor variety rather than more weight, with Pomona focused in elegance, sweeter and more fruit-forward, and the Riserva showing more power and a sense of minerality in the classic traditional style.

Il Poggione

*

Loc. Monteano, S. Angelo in Colle, 53024 Montalcino (SI)

(39) 05778 44029

Fabrizio Bindocci

info@ilpoggione.it

www.tenutailpoggione.it

Brunello Di Montalcino

Brunello di Montalcino

140 ha; 600,000 bottles
[map p. 90]

Il Poggione has been in the Franceschi family since the nineteenth century. It was originally the Fattorio St. Angelo; the name changed in 1956 when the two brothers who were the current owners split their estate into Il Poggione and Col d'Orcia. (Col d'Orcia was subsequently sold to the Cinzano family). The winery buildings form a complex about 2 km below St. Angelo, down a steep unpaved road. The winery was built in 2004, and is much larger than it appears, with a vast fermentation hall behind the offices, and separate halls with botti and tonneaux underground. It's is in the center of the vineyards, and is partly built into the hillside. Before it was built, the wine was made in a series of buildings in the village.

The vineyards form something of an amphitheater, part of a 600 ha estate which also includes 12,000 olive trees, and are ringed by mountains to the west. "We are aware that to make great wines you need old vines and we have some of the oldest vineyards in the region. We never uproot old vineyards, but we replace individual vines. One of the things we are proud of is that Il Poggione ages well, for up to twenty years," says winemaker Fabrizio Bindocci. "We consider ourselves a traditional producer, but open to technology."

Rosso and Brunello are each about a third of production. The Brunello and the Riserva are aged only in 52 hl botti of French oak. "The botti are not toasted," Fabrizio explains. "Brunello spends 3 years in botti, Riserva spends 4 years, so we don't want oak influence to be strong. New barrels would be too strong. Barriques tends to homogenize wine; we don't want to adapt our wine to consumers, we want consumers to appreciate our wine. We want to maintain typicity, we want to make wine that you can see comes from this region. The botti allow Sangiovese to evolve over years of aging."

The regular Rosso, which is intended for consumption sooner, is aged mostly in botti, with 20-30% in tonneaux, and makes a nicely restrained impression. "We've always taken the view that we should make a serious Rosso," Fabrizio says. It comes partly from specific vineyards and partly from young vines in Brunello vineyards. A second Rosso, Leopoldo Franceschi, is a barrel selection, aged mostly in tonneaux, and is more of a young Brunello. The Brunello gives a mineral impression of black fruits and usually needs some time. "When our Brunello is released, it may not be as pleasant as wines aged in barriques, but it will age longer," Fabrizio says. The Riserva, Vigna Paganelli, comes from the oldest vines, a 12 ha vineyard planted in 1964, and shows the concentration of old vines with a smooth palate of black fruits, moving in a more chocolaty direction than the regular Brunello; it is not so much more powerful as smoother and deeper. These are very fine wines, but patience is required.

Castello Romitorio

*

 Loc. Romitorio, 53024 Montalcino (SI)

 (39) 05778 47212

 info@castelloromitorio.com

 www.castelloromitorio.com

 Brunello Di Montalcino

 Brunello di Montalcino

 15 ha; 150,000 bottles

[map p. 90]

Castello Romitorio takes its name from a twelfth century fortress in the northwest quadrant of Montalcino. Two thirds of the vineyards are in the vicinity of the winery, and the other third are at Poggio di Sopra, near Castelnuovo dell'Abate in the southeast. The striking paintings on the labels reflect ownership by artist Sandro Chia, who purchased the estate in 1984 and planted vineyards largely with Sangiovese. The additional vineyards at Poggio di Sopra were added in 1990. Famed oenologist Carlo Ferrini is a consultant.

The hierarchy of Sangiovese varietal wines ascends from Chianti Colle Senesi (which spends six months in Slavonian oak), to Rosso di Montalcino (12 months in French barriques), and Brunello di Montalcino (12 months in French barriques and 12 months in Slavonian oak). The Riserva comes from a single vineyard, and spends 36 months in a mixture of French and Slavonian oak, and the top Brunello is the Filo di Seta, which is based on selection of the best lots, and spends 30 months in French barriques.

The house is a modernist and the style is refined: the Brunello is relatively light, but Filo di Seta moves up a notch with more structure evident in the background and an increased sense of precision. The Riserva is deeper and rounder, but still in the elegant style of the house. There's also a Sant'Antimo blend of Sangiovese, Cabernet Sauvignon, and Canaiolo, and an IGT Toscana Bordeaux blend, as well as a white blend of Vermentino and Chardonnay. Another estate in Maremma was purchased in the mid nineties.

Salvioni

***

Piazza Cavour, 19, 53024 Montalcino (SI)

(39) 05778 48499

Alessia Salvioni

info@aziendasalvioni.com

www.aziendasalvioni.com

Brunello Di Montalcino

Brunello di Montalcino

4 ha; 12,000 bottles

[map p. 90]

The tiny scale of production at La Cerbaiola is indicated by its aging cellar, underneath the family house in Piazza Cavour in the town of Montalcino: it has 6 botti of 20 hl. That's the total production for one of the mythic producers of Montalcino. The property at La Cerbaiola, three vineyards totaling 4 ha in a 20 ha estate immediately adjacent to Cerbaiona, has been in the Salvioni family for three generations, but winemaking is relatively recent.

"Our story started in 1985 when my father decided to make wine," says Alessia Salvioni. Giulio Salvioni's first vintage in 1985 was an immediate success: the traditional approach, using indigenous yeast, botti (albeit of medium size), and lack of filtration, marked the wines firmly in the artisanal camp. The entire vineyard is declared for Brunello, but some is declassified to Rosso when the crop is unusually large or there is a poor vintage. There are certainly ups and downs in production. In 2012 there were 12,000 bottles of Brunello, in 2013 there were only four botti (about 10,000 bottles), in 2014 the entire crop was declassified to Rosso, and in 2015 there will probably be 15,000 bottles, all Brunello. The wines have that combination of full flavor and density, yet elegant expression, that marks the vineyards of Cerbaiola and Cerbaiona.

San Filippo *

Loc. *San Filippo 134, 53024 Montalcino, (SI)*

(39) 05778 47176

Roberto Giannelli

info@sanfilippomontalcino.com

www.sanfilippomontalcino.com

Brunello Di Montalcino

Brunello di Montalcino, Le Lucère

10 ha; 65,000 bottles

[map p. 90]

"I was in real estate and fifteen years ago I was asked to help sell the winery. I ended up buying it myself," says Roberto Gianelli. "I changed everything, the first five years were difficult." The winery occupies a group of buildings at the end of a track that winds down from the main road to San Filippo, where there are half a dozen producers. Dating from 1977, this is one of the older established wineries in Montalcino. The vineyards, all in San Filippo, were planted in the seventies, so the oldest vines are now almost fifty years old.

All wines are DOC, ranging from the Rosso di Montalcino (coming from dedicated vineyards) to the Brunello and the Le Lucère single vineyard of the oldest vines (also produced as a Riserva in top vintages). Are you a traditionalist or a modernist, I asked Roberto? "Oh, for me it's the grapes that matter. We have both large oak and small oak. Brunello ages in large oak, the single vineyard ages 14 months in each small and large oak, Riserva has an extra six months all in barriques. Maybe we are more traditionalist than new. We look for good fruits, fermentation that isn't too long or aggressive, maximum of 20 days on the skin. We want a clean style with good aromas, not too aggressive. In general we have soft wine, not too powerful."

The Rosso is quite light and fresh, the Brunello is more serious but remains relatively soft, and the single vineyard Lucère shows the style to best effect, a deeper, richer version of the Brunello, but elegant rather than powerful, poised between savory and chocolaty. The style to me seems to veer increasingly in a modernist direction along the range.

Sassodisole *

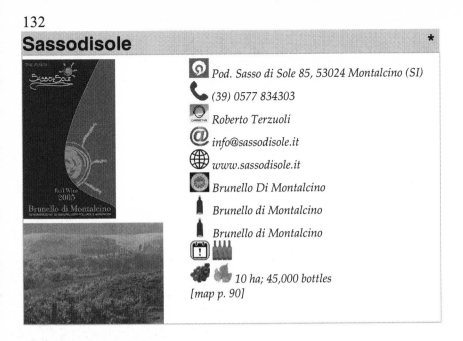

Pod. *Sasso di Sole 85, 53024 Montalcino (SI)*

(39) 0577 834303

Roberto Terzuoli

info@sassodisole.it

www.sassodisole.it

Brunello Di Montalcino

Brunello di Montalcino

Brunello di Montalcino

10 ha; 45,000 bottles

[*map p. 90*]

Sassodisole is a new name for an old estate. Originally it was owned by two brothers, who split their holdings 25 years ago. The Terzuoli family has been involved in agriculture since the seventeenth century; Bruno and Graziella Terzuoli moved into winemaking during the 1970s, and Sassodisole is run today by their grandson Roberto, who worked at Biondi-Santi before taking over the estate. (The neighboring estate, Santa Giulia, is the other half of the original property.)

Vineyards are in a series of slopes all around the cellar, facing south or southwest, at 350m. The small winery is stuffed with modern equipment. There is a stylish tasting room, where you may be greeted by manager Lorenzo Moscatelli, who is Roberto's sole assistant in the winery. "We are a traditional producer," Lorenzo explains, "we use only 35hl or 50 hl botti of Slavonian oak for aging."

The estate is located in the far northeast corner of Montalcino, where it overlaps with the Orcia DOC. The focus is exclusively on Sangiovese. The entry level wine is Orcia Rosso, which comes from the youngest vines; the size of the estate was more or less doubled when 4 ha were planted to make the Orcia. A sparkling rosé was introduced in 2016, also coming from this vineyard. The Rosso di Montalcino and Brunello come from the original vineyards. The Riserva is based on selection. "Usually the best grapes come from the top of the hill. We harvest first for the Brunello and then go back three or four days later to harvest the smallest berries and bunches. This means we have to decide at harvest whether to select for the Riserva," Lorenzo says.

The Orcia Rosso spend 4-5 months in oak, the Rosso di Montalcino spends 8-9 months, but Brunellos have extended aging. "Brunello ages for 3 years, Riserva for 4 years, so we need very light wood," says Lorenzo. The Orcia is a nice summer wine showing light red fruits, the Rosso is slightly deeper and has more fruit complexity and a little restraint, the Brunello adds a sense of structure to the smooth sheen of the fruits, and there is a sense of minerality to the Riserva. Overall the style is elegant rather than powerful. "We follow the same style for all the wines, I think we can see the same hand, the same philosophy, in all our wines," Lorenzo says.

Tenuta Silvio Nardi ★

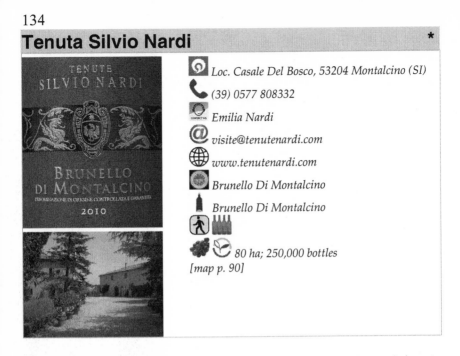

⊙ *Loc. Casale Del Bosco, 53204 Montalcino (SI)*

📞 *(39) 0577 808332*

👤 *Emilia Nardi*

@ *visite@tenutenardi.com*

🌐 *www.tenutenardi.com*

◼ *Brunello Di Montalcino*

🍷 *Brunello Di Montalcino*

🚶 🏭

🍇 ⌚ *80 ha; 250,000 bottles*

[map p. 90]

Silvio Nardi purchased the Casale del Bosco estate in 1950, and then in 1962 purchased the Manachiara estate. Silvio's daughter, Emilia, has been in charge of the estate since 1990; the consulting oenologist is Eric Boissenot from Bordeaux. Casale del Bosco is to the west, and Manachiara is to the east of Montalcino. The fruit from Casale del Bosco tends to elegance, whereas Manachiara is riper. The combination anticipated the later trend of blending between north and south. About half the vineyards are in each of the estates, with a total of 36 different plots. The Rosso comes from the Casale del Bosco estate, the Brunello is a blend from Casale del Bosco and Manchiara, while Manachiara is a single vineyard wine from old vines, and Poggio Doria comes from a vineyard in the northwest corner of Casale del Bosco. The overall impression is modern but not ultra modern.

Talenti

*

Podere Pian Di Conte, 53020 Sant'Angelo in Colle (SI)

(39) 0577 844064

Riccardo Talenti

info@talentimontalcino.it

www.talentimontalcino.it

Brunello Di Montalcino

Brunello Di Montalcino

21 ha; 100,000 bottles
[map p. 90]

Pierluigi Talenti founded this estate in 1980, and today it is run by Riccardo Talenti. The property is in the hills opposite the village of Sant'Angelo in Colle. The heart is in the Brunellos. Vinification is similar for the Rosso, Brunello, and Riserva: fermentation in stainless steel is followed by aging in a mix of French tonneaux (500 liter barrels) and Slavonian botti, the basic difference being the length of aging. The Rosso comes from the younger vineyards (less than 15 years of age), the Brunello from vineyards over 20 years, and the Riserva from the 2 ha Paretaio vineyard. The approach is modern, but in a lighter style. Fresh but showing some structure to the black fruits, the Rosso previews the Brunello, which is a little smoother and more structured; the Riserva shows greater refinement rather than more power. There are also two IGTs: Trefolo, a blend of Sangiovese, Syrah, and Canaiolo, and Rispolla, a blend of 40% Cabernet Sauvignon, 30% Merlot, and 30% Petit Verdot. They are not very flexible about appointments, so make arrangements to visit well in advance.

Val di Suga

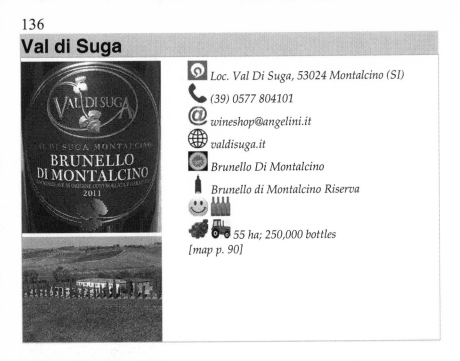

Loc. Val Di Suga, 53024 Montalcino (SI)

(39) 0577 804101

wineshop@angelini.it

valdisuga.it

Brunello Di Montalcino

Brunello di Montalcino Riserva

55 ha; 250,000 bottles

[map p. 90]

Val de Suga was founded in the 1970s, and its ownership has changed as it has passed through various conglomerate mergers. It became part of Tenimenti Angelini in 1994 when privately-owned pharmaceutical company Angelini simultaneously bought Val di Suga in Montalcino, Tre Rose in Montepulciano, and San Leonino in Chianti Classico. Then in 2011 Angelini bought Bertani, the well known producer in Valpolicella. In 2014 all of the estates were united under the banner of Bertani domains. It's probably fair to say that all of these domains are mid-range: they achieve a certain reliability in quality, but rarely scale the heights.

Since Angelini bought Val di Suga, however, there has been investment in vineyards and cellar. The focus is exclusively in Brunello, with the range ascending from the Rosso, to the Brunello, to the Riserva, and three single vineyard wines, Poggio al Granchio, Vigna Spuntali, and Vigna del Lago, which represent distinct areas (southeast, southwest, and north, near the winery). The Brunello is aged mostly in botti, but the single vineyard wines see new barriques, and age as long as Riserva although not labeled as such. From Rosso to Brunello to single vineyard, the style is light and quite attractive, with intensity increasing along the series, but not offering the prospect of increasing complexity with age. The single vineyard wines are definitely in the modern idiom, but are over-oaked for my palate, and I worry about their aging capacity. Vigna Spuntali is closest in style to the Riserva, then the sense of oak builds with Poggio al Granchio and finally Vigna del Largo.

Valdicava ***

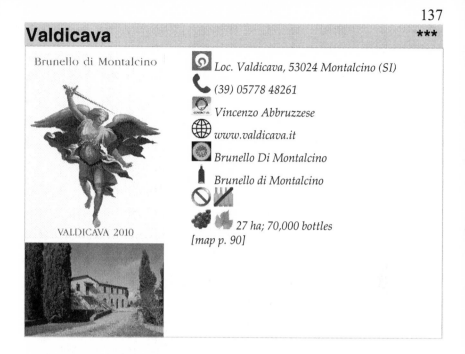

Brunello di Montalcino

VALDICAVA 2010

⊙ Loc. Valdicava, 53024 Montalcino (SI)

📞 (39) 05778 48261

Vincenzo Abbruzzese

🌐 www.valdicava.it

Brunello Di Montalcino

⚑ Brunello di Montalcino

🚫 ▨

🍇 🍇 27 ha; 70,000 bottles

[map p. 90]

When I visited Valdicava, we had to go a long way round to the back entrance, because the front was blocked by massive reconstruction works. Driving through the extensive estate on the way to the winery, we passed the Madonna del Piano, a small building that used to be a church, and which is just above the famous 8 ha vineyard of its name. The work is to build a new winery, a stable for the racing horses (another interest), and a tasting room. The present winery is small facility, packed with equipment and botti.

One of the older established producers in Montalcino, Valdicava was turned into something of a cult wine after Vincenzo Abbruzzese took over in 1987. The estate was founded by his grandfather, Bramante Abbruzzese, in 1953. Valdicava was a founding member of the Consorzio, and has been bottling wine under the Valdicava label since 1977 (previously they carried a generic description from the Consorzio with the winery's name). The vineyards occupy only a small part of the 135 ha estate, located in the northeast quadrant (and extending into Montosoli), where the most powerful wines of Montalcino are produced.

Valdicava produces three wines: Rosso (from the youngest vines), Brunello, and the single vineyard Madonna del Piano Riserva, produced only in the best vintages in small amounts (around 800 cases). Wines are aged only in botti, which are natural wood with no toast. The style is forceful, and at all levels the wines give an impression of the density that comes from low yields (in fact some of the lowest in the region), and the wines correspondingly need time to come around. Although forceful, Valdicava does not lose elegance and purity of fruits. Madonna is not so much more intense than Valdicava as different in its profile, with an intriguing blend of minerality on the bouquet and chocolate on the finish. "It's different but it's just between the other vineyards, there must be something in the soil." Its character comes right through vintage variation, but it needs a long time to come around, perhaps twenty years. How long will these wines age? Vincenzo has been quoted as saying, "I guarantee the Riserva for the lifetime of the buyer."

Bolgheri

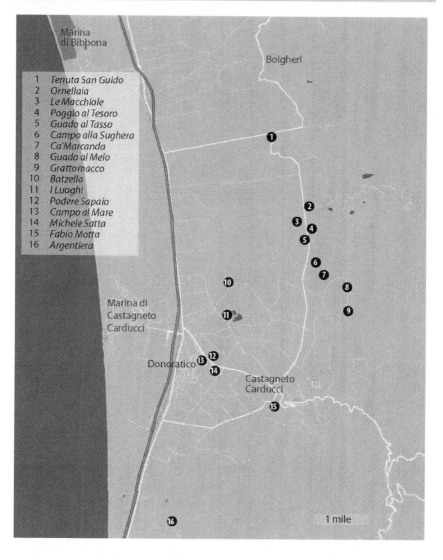

1 Tenuta San Guido
2 Ornellaia
3 Le Macchiole
4 Poggio al Tesoro
5 Guado al Tasso
6 Campo alla Sughera
7 Ca'Marcanda
8 Guado al Melo
9 Grattomacco
10 Batzella
11 I Luoghi
12 Podere Sapaio
13 Campo al Mare
14 Michele Satta
15 Fabio Motta
16 Argentiera

Batzella

Località Badia 227, 57022 Castagneto Carducci (LI)

(39) 0565 775776

Franco Batzella

info@batzella.com

www.batzella.com

Bolgheri

Bolgheri, Tam

8 ha; 55,000 bottles

[map p. 139]

Batzella is a boutique operation. I'm not sure if it is the smallest producer in Bolgheri, but it must be one of the smallest. Khanh Nguyen and Franco Batzella worked at the World Bank until they decided to retire early and do something different. Initially they decided to start in Montalcino. "Since no one knew us and we were starting without any reputation, we thought we should start somewhere that had a reputation," says Khanh, who makes the wines. They bought and planted an estate in Montalcino, and started selling the grapes, but then 8 ha became available in Bolgheri, and they decided this was more attractive because of the way the region was expanding. They have 1 ha of Cabernet Franc, 1 ha Syrah, 1 ha white varieties, and 5 ha Cabernet Sauvignon, planted with 6 different clones. The first year of production was 2003.

There are three levels of wine: a Bolgheri Superiore, a Bolgheri, and an entry-level wine. Yields are slightly lower for Tâm, a blend of 60% Cabernet Sauvignon with 40% Cabernet Franc, which is the top of the line Bolgheri Superiore and spends two years in barriques, than for the Bolgheri DOC Peàn, which has 70% Cabernet Sauvignon and 30% Cabernet Franc, and spends one year in barriques. This is really an artisan operation, in semi-permanent surroundings because of problems obtaining a construction permit, which has finally come through. "It proves you don't need a cathedral to make good wine," says Franco.

Ca' Marcanda ★★

📍 *Loc. Santa Teresa 272, 57022 Castagneto Carducci (LI)*

📞 *(39) 0565 763809*

👤 *Gaia Gaja*

@ *info@camarcanda.com*

⬤ Bolgheri

🍷 *Bolgheri, Camarcanda*

🚫 🔧

🍇🍇 *120 ha; 450,000 bottles*

[map p. 139]

Angelo Gaja is a force of nature—and not one to do things by halves. Famous for his Barbaresco (and Barolo), where his single vineyard wines are at the top of the hierarchy, he expanded into Montalcino by acquiring the Pieve Santa Restituta vineyards in 1994. Having decided he wanted also to make wine in Bolgheri, he conducted a long and patient search until he identified the best terroirs. "It was difficult when I came here because there was no historical record, all the new vineyards were planted in land that was not vineyards before. Although I am not a Burgundian, land is important for me, so I investigated. There was research done in 1987 to discover whether there was land similar to Sassicaia. They transferred the research to a big map, with a harlequin of color codes. I asked a friend, a producer, to look at it with me. I asked him, what is the color of Sassicaia's land, he showed me the yellow, and there was yellow also at Ornellaia and Guado al Tasso."

There was another yellow patch, and Angelo set out to buy the land, after a lengthy wooing process, he was able to purchase the vineyards in 1996. "I visited seventeen times, making many different proposals to rent the land from two brothers, and my wife said, 'You are losing time, these are Ca'Marcanda people' (this means endless negotiations without ever signing a deal). But the eighteenth time their sister was with the two brothers, I had not met her before, she said that renting did not make sense, so why don't we sell it to Mr. Gaja?"

Ca'Marcanda became the name of the winery. There were some small plots of Vermentino and Sangiovese, but most of the land was given over to other crops or was unplanted. "So what to plant? I know the area has an avocation for Cabernet, I tasted the wine of Sassicaia, but I didn't like to make a wine that would be a copy of Sassicaia. So we decided on our own blend, it's a Bordeaux blend but in the mind of the artisan I would like to make a wine that follows *our* ideas, that speaks the Tuscan language." Planting started in 1997. "Every year we planted 7-8 ha, in 2010 we reached 100 ha," says Angelo. "We plan a maximum of 120 ha," he says, explaining that this is more or less the limit he sees for artisan production.

A striking new winery has been built, largely underground. There are three wines. Promis is a blend of Merlot and Syrah, with a little Sangiovese; Magari is half Merlot with a quarter each of Cabernet Sauvignon and Cabernet Franc; and Camarcanda is half Merlot with 40% Cabernet Sauvignon and 10% Cabernet Franc. Production is around 25,000 cases of Promis, 8,000 of Magari, and 2,500 of Camarcanda. The wines typify Bolgheri in their combination of underlying structure with superficial lushness; Promis is always the most forward, " Magari is the flagship of the winery that best matches food," says Angelo, and Camarcanda is the most elegant and structured, with an impression that it has more than the actual 40% of Cabernet Sauvignon.

Campo alla Sughera *

Localita' Caccia al Piano 280, 57022 Bolgheri, Castagneto Carducci (LI)

(39) 0565 766911

Rita Tonini

info@campoallasughera.com

www.campoallasughera.com

Bolgheri

Bolgheri, Arnione

16 ha; 110,000 bottles

[map p. 139]

This is something of a lifestyle winery, founded in 1998 by Baldwin Knauf, a magnate in construction. The first vintage was 2001. The flagship wine is Arnione, initially a blend of Cabernet Sauvignon and Merlot with a little Petit Verdot, and since 2006 also Cabernet Franc. A typical blend for current vintages is up to half Cabernet Sauvignon, with equal amounts of Merlot and Cabernet Franc, and a smaller amount of Petit Verdot. Adèo is the second wine, a blend of Cabernet Sauvignon and Merlot. Both have a full, oak-driven style. The white Archenio is largely Vermentino.

Podere Grattamacco (ColleMassari) **

Grattamacco

BOLGHERI SUPERIORE
DENOMINAZIONE DI ORIGINE CONTROLLATA

Imbottigliato all'origine da
Collemassari Spa Società Agricola
nel Podere Grattamacco
Castagneto Carducci, Italia
Product of Italy

Località Lungagnano 129, 57022 Castagneto Carducci (LI)

(39) 0565 765069

Michela Bartalini

grattamacco@collemassari.it

www.collemassari.it

Bolgheri

IGT Toscana, L'Alberello

16 ha; 120,000 bottles
[map p. 139]

One of the earliest estates to be founded in Bolgheri—in fact the second, after Sassicaia—Grattamacco has remained influential since its establishment in 1977, when the idea of basing wine on Cabernet Sauvignon was still novel. Founder Piermario Meletti Cavallari ran the estate for a quarter century until he sold it to Swiss company Colle Massari, owned by Claudia Tipa, who also owns Poggio di Sotto in Montalcino and Castello Colle-Massari in Montecucco. Piermario Meletti Cavallari continued to live at Grattamacco, but now makes wine on Elba. Grattamacco is located between Bolgheri and Castegneto Carducci, on an elevation of about 100 m, basically on a plain that gets steady breezes. About half of the 34 ha estate is planted with vineyards or olive groves; the rest is uncultivated Mediterranean shrubs. Grattamacco is a blend of Cabernet Sauvignon, Merlot, and Sangiovese (which in this windy location avoids the problems of humidity that occur elsewhere in Bolgheri. L'Alberello comes from a 2 ha plot planted with Cabernet Sauvignon, Cabernet Franc, and Petit Verdot; the name reflects the unusual training of the vines very high in the alberello style. There is also a white from Vermentino. The winemaker today is Lucca Marone, aided by consulting enologist Maurizio Castelli.

Guado al Tasso ★★

Trada Provinciale Bolgherese, 57020 Bolgheri (LI)

☎ *(39) 055 23595*

Marco Ferrarese

@ *antinori@antinori.it*

⊕ *www.antinori.it/en/26-generazioni/guado-al-tasso*

Bolgheri

Bolgheri, Guado al Tasso

300 ha; 800,000 bottles

[map p. 139]

Guado al Tasso is part of Antinori's Florentine Empire, which has estates all over Tuscany and Umbria. In addition to several estates in Chianti, there are estates in Montalcino and Orvieto. Antinori's most important super-Tuscans are Tignanello (Sangiovese based but historically the first wine to blend in Cabernet Sauvignon), Solaia (Cabernet based, coming from the Tignanello estate in Chianti), and Guado al Tasso (the super-Tuscan from Bolgheri). Some of the production at Guado al Tasso is transferred to make the Villa Antinori IGT Toscana.

The long road up to Al Tasso—it runs all the way from the main road near the coast to the Strada Bolgherese (Strada del Vino) close to the eastern boundary—is lined with olive trees. In addition to the home vineyard, extending all around the road, there are further vineyards at the northern and southern edges of Bolgheri. The total vineyard area of 300 ha is planted to 100 ha Cabernet Sauvignon, 40 ha Merlot, 50 ha Syrah, 20 ha Cabernet Franc, 5 ha Petit Verdot, and 40 ha Vermentino (close to the sea). The approach to terroir is quite Bordelais: Cabernet Sauvignon, Cabernet Franc, and Merlot are planted with increasing proportions of clay. There are also 200 ha of cereal (some of this is used to feed their pigs) and 1,000 olive trees.

The eponymous Guado al Tasso and a second wine, Il Brucciato, use different dedicated vineyard plots, with 80 ha presently used for Brucciato and 60 ha for Al Tasso. Guado al Tasso is usually about 60% Cabernet Sauvignon, 20-30% Merlot, 10-15% Cabernet Franc, and 1-2% Petit Verdot. Il Brucciato has about 40% Cabernet Sauvignon, with Merlot and Syrah. "The Syrah makes Il Brucciato more forward; in fact there was some in Al Tasso until 2007. Syrah is for us an excellent variety but with Cabernet Franc we have more elegance and longevity. Syrah in Bolgheri is often too exuberant, and Al Tasso we want to get the elegance," says winemaker Marco Ferrarese.

Guado al Tasso is harvested at yields of 20-25 hl/ha, lower than Il Brucciato, which is about 40-45 hl/ha. There's a small amount of declassification from Guado al Tasso to Il Brucciato, usually less than 5%. Production is about 8,000 cases of Guado al Tasso and 25,000 cases of Il Brucciato. Guado Al Tasso seems to vary from warm vintages where it shows the softness that is typical of Bolgheri to cooler vintages where the Cabernet character comes out more directly, but it always has a pleasing sense of restraint.

Le Macchiole ⁕⁕

LE MACCHIOLE
BOLGHERI

BOLGHERI ROSSO

📍 Via Bolgherese 189/a, Bolgheri (LI)

📞 (39) 0565 766092

👤 Cinzia Merli

@ info@lemacchiole.it

🌐 www.lemacchiole.it

Bolgheri

IGT Toscana, Paleo Rosso

🍇⌚ 27 ha; 170,000 bottles
[map p. 139]

This estate has an unusual origin, as it indigenous to Bolgheri, instead of being formed by outsiders. It started when Eugenio Campolmi extended his experience producing wine for his father's restaurant into purchasing a vineyard and producing wine commercially. Le Macchiole was founded in 1982, relatively early in the history of Bolgheri; the first wine was produced in 1987. After Eugenio's death in 2002, it continued to be run by his wife, Cinzia Merli. The winery found its focus on producing monovarietal wines from international varieties. Paleo Rosso started as a Bordeaux blend in 1989, but by 2001 it became a monovarietal Cabernet Franc, quite a revolutionary act at the time. Scrio was introduced as a monovarietal Syrah in 1994. Messorio, a monovarietal Merlot, has been the signature wine ever since its introduction in 1994. Le Macchiole's simple Bolgheri Rosso is somewhat of a second wine, coming from younger vines; the blend has changed with time, and now has Merlot, Cabernet Franc, and Syrah. There is also a white, Paleo Bianco (Chardonnay and Sauvignon Blanc) These are not wines for instant gratification, but need some time to get out from under the oak and to express themselves.

Tenuta Dell'Ornellaia ★★★

Via Bolgherese, 191, 57020 Bolgheri (LI)

(39) 0565 71811

Axel Heinz

info@ornellaia.it

www.ornellaia.com

Bolgheri

Bolgheri, Ornellaia

112 ha; 950,000 bottles

[map p. 139]

Close to the Sassicaia estate, Ornellaia became one of the great names in Bolgheri almost immediately after it was established in 1981 and produced its first vintage in 1985. It was created by Marchese Lodovico Antinori, younger brother of Marchese Piero Antinori of the wine producer Marchese Antinori. The Mondavi winery of California took a minority interest in the estate in 1999, acquired the entire estate in 2002 and went into partnership with the Frescobaldi family; and then Frescobaldi purchased the estate outright in 2005 after Constellation Brands took over Mondavi.

Ornellaia has two separate vineyards: the home estate around the winery; and the Bellaria vineyard just a little to the south (planted between 1992 and 2005). Today four wines are produced. The top two are Ornellaia itself, and the 100% Merlot produced from the Masseto hill. A second wine, La Serre Nuove, was introduced in 1997, and is made by declassifying lots from Ornellaia. "There's a limit to how much great Ornellaia can be made; we do not need to create scarcity as is done in Bordeaux by diverting to the second wine," says winemaker Axel Heinz. Le Volte is more a separate blend (of Sangiovese with Cabernet Sauvignon and Merlot) than a third wine, since it includes purchased grapes.

Ornellaia's varietal composition has changed somewhat over the years. The original intention of a blend of Cabernet Sauvignon with Merlot was somewhat sidetracked when the Merlot from the Masseto hill (which is planted exclusively with Merlot) was diverted into a separate cuvée because it was so good. "Merlot can soak up water from the soil, that is probably the secret of Merlot at Masseto, and why it isn't jammy and over ripe," Axel explains. Masseto prices higher than Ornellaia, and there are plans to separate it by building another winery. Merlot increased in the blend after the vineyards at Bellaria (a slightly cooler site exposed more to the sea) was acquired. Having peaked at almost a third of the blend, now it is back down to around a quarter. Cabernet Sauvignon was around 80% for the first decade, then dropped abruptly to 65% with the 1997 vintage, but for the past few years has been only just above half; it's dropped a little recently as the result of a replanting program. Perhaps reflecting the warmer climate, Cabernet Franc has been increasing (5% in the first vintages, 15-20% in recent years) and Petit Verdot has been included since 2003. "The tendency is for warm years to use less Merlot and more Cabernet Franc," Axel explains. The grapes for Ornellaia come roughly half from the home vineyard and half from Bellaria. Ornellaia's level of production has been fairly steady, something over 8,000 cases, although production of La Serre Nuove has increased from 2,500 to 12,500 cases since its inception.

Tenuta San Guido ***

SASSICAIA

2012

BOLGHERI SASSICAIA

Tenuta San Guido - Castagneto Carducci - Italia

750 ml ℮   PRODOTTO IN ITALIA   13,5% vol

⊚ *Loc. Le Capanne n. 27, 57020 Bolgheri, Castagneto Carducci (LI)*

☎ *(39) 0565 762003*

Carlo Paoli

@ *info@sassicaia.com*

⊕ *www.sassicaia.com*

⦾ *Bolgheri*

▮ *Bolgheri Sassicaia*

⊘ 🏭

🍇 🚜 *103 ha; 800,000 bottles*

[map p. 139]

Sassicaia stands alone. It's the only wine in Italy to have its own DOC. "Sassicaia was Vino da Tavola until 1994 when we got the DOC. Until that time the proportion of Cabernet Sauvignon and Cabernet Franc was 85:15, so when we had to decide regulations for the DOC we decided 80% should be Cabernet Sauvignon and the rest could be anything," says the Marquis Incisa. It is no longer the most expensive super-Tuscan, perhaps because it has not moved in the direction of power and extraction, but has remained true to its original objective of an elegant wine in the tradition of Bordeaux's left bank, although necessarily more Mediterranean than Atlantic in style.

Reflecting on changes over time, the Marquis Incisa says, "There is a little difference (in alcohol levels). Twenty years ago it was difficult to get 12%, today we try keep it as low as possible. People say we are picking the grapes too early. People have been reducing yields because they thought it makes higher quality, but this then makes the wine unbalanced. Sassicaia started at 60 hl/ha, when everything else was generally around 100 hl/ha. Some people went down to 30 hl/ha but this makes it very difficult to contain the alcohol."

The main change has been the move to introduce a second wine. "Until 2000 we made only one wine. We were using 98-100% of our grapes. Since 2000 we have made another wine, and we select. The reason we started making Guidalberto was that we didn't want to increase the production of Sassicaia. The wines with the highest ratings in American journals were all based on Merlot so we thought we must make a wine with Merlot to follow the trend." Guidalberto is 60% Cabernet Sauvignon to 40% Merlot; it comes mostly from specific vineyards, but about 20% comes from grapes declassified from Sassicaia. There is also another wine, Le Diffese, a blend of Cabernet Sauvignon and Sangiovese from the Guidalberto vineyard, "but it's not really a third wine, it's a different wine."

Michele Satta **

Loc. *Vigna Al Cavalière 61, 57020 Castagneto Carducci (LI)*

📞 *(39) 0565 773 041*

Fabio Motta

@ *info@michelesatta.com*

🌐 *www.michelesatta.com*

⬤ Bolgheri

🍾 Bolgheri, I Castagni

20 ha; 150,000 bottles

[map p. 139]

One of the pioneers in Bolgheri, Michele Satta started in 1982 with only 4 ha, "but it wasn't a project, he moved slowly into wine production," said Fabio Motta, his son-in-law, an oenologue who was in charge of marketing until he started his own winery (see mini-profile). Today the home vineyard occupies 25 ha at the southern limit of the Bolgheri region. Its gradual development has been responsible for the higgledy piggledy organization of many varieties across the vineyards. Standing at one spot in the vineyard, I could see Cabernet Sauvignon, Merlot, Syrah, Teroldego, Vermentino, and Viognier. Overall, plantings are 30% Cabernet Sauvignon, 30% Merlot, 20% Sangiovese, 10% Syrah, 10% Teroldego, but I Castagni focuses on 70% Cabernet Sauvignon, 20% Syrah, and 10% Teroldego.

"I Castagni started with only Cabernet Sauvignon and Merlot. After Michele decided to make a single vineyard wine, he decided to add Syrah and Teroldego. Originally when Michele planted the vineyard he felt he must plant Cabernet Sauvignon because the area is in Bolgheri, but he also wanted to plant his favorite grapes, Syrah and Teroldego. Teroldego has rich color and lots of tannins, but is very soft. This was planted rather than Merlot because ripening is very slow. Probably the Syrah will increase in future," says Fabio. Michele has been an enthusiast for Syrah ever since visiting the northern Rhône, and he introduced a varietal Syrah with the 2007 vintage.

The small winery is on the edge of the home vineyard. It's quite unassuming, with plans to build a second storey with a tasting room, but in true Alice in Wonderland fashion, this has been stuck in the bureaucracy because of fears that carbon dioxide (notably heavier than air) might rise up and kill the patrons. In the meantime, Michele continues to make wine in a traditional manner; no modern gimmicks here.

Poggio al Tesoro
*

Via del Fosso 33, 57022 Donoratico, Castagneto
Carducci (LI)

(39) 0565 7731051

poggioaltesoro@poggioaltesoro.it

www.poggioaltesoro.it

Bolgheri

Bolgheri, Sondraia

Bolgheri, Solasole

65 ha; 330,000 bottles
[map p. 139]

Poggio al Tesoro is a project of Allegrini, one of the best and largest producers in Valpolicella, who expanded into Bolgheri in 2002 (and into Montalcino by purchasing San Polo in 2008: see mini-profile). The estate has three vineyards, Via Bolgherese, Le Grottine, and Le Sondraia. The style is typically rich. "Poggio al Tesoro always harvests very late," says Marilisa Allegrini. The signature wine is Sondraia, about two thirds Cabernet Sauvignon with 25% Merlot and 10% Cabernet Franc, matured in an equal mix of new and one-year barriques. It gives an impression of having more Cabernet Franc than it really does, but apparently this is due to the special qualities of the Merlot in this location. Dedicato a Walter, named for Walter Allegrini, is a 100% Cabernet Franc that brings out a full, chocolaty expression of varietal character. Medittera is Syrah with some Merlot and Cabernet Sauvignon. The white wine, Solosole, was part of the start of a trend to grow Vermentino in Bolgheri. "I didn't want to make the standard Italian white. It comes from a special clone originating in Corsica," says Marilisa. Far from the often amorphous character of the variety, it conveys fresh and herbal impressions with depth on the palate.

Maremma

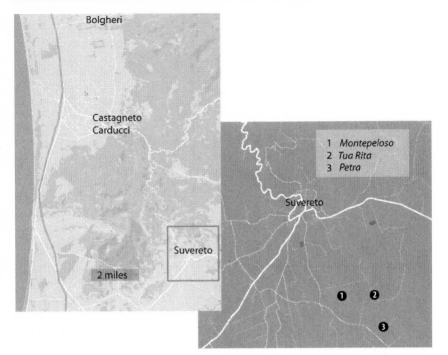

Montepeloso **

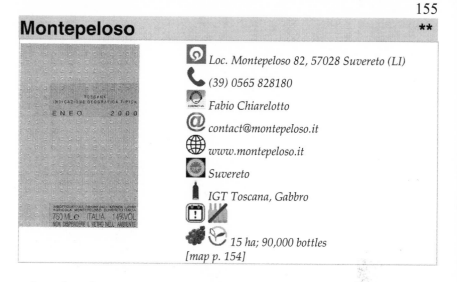

Loc. *Montepeloso 82, 57028 Suvereto (LI)*

(39) 0565 828180

Fabio Chiarelotto

contact@montepeloso.it

www.montepeloso.it

Suvereto

IGT Toscana, Gabbro

15 ha; 90,000 bottles
[*map p. 154*]

Fabio Chiarelotto grew up in Switzerland; Suvereto is his mother's native place. He purchased Montepeloso in 1995, starting with 9 ha on the Montepeloso hill and then added another 5 ha on the facing Fontanella hill. Things have turned out a little differently from what he expected. "When I bought the estate the wine was mainly Sangiovese, with some Cabernet and white varieties. My idea was to make an Italian wine, I wanted to shape an Italian Tuscan blend, I wanted to get away from Sangiovese pumped up with Merlot." But the wine that has made Montepeloso famous is Cabernet Sauvignon.

"When we purchased the winery and tasted the separate Cabernet lots, we were impressed by how complete the Cabernet was. So I felt that since there was no real history here, I would start with Cabernet, get a reputation, and then work on the Italian project." He makes four wines: the Gabbro Cabernet Sauvignon, Nardo, which is mostly Sangiovese, the Eneo Sangiovese-based blend, and the entry-level A Quo. The blends in Nardo and Eneo have been moving towards the Italian project, to blend Montepulciano, Sangiovese, Alicante, and Marselan (a cross of Cabernet Sauvignon with Grenache). Gabbro, the top wine, spends 18 months in oak (85-90% new). "I tried a little Cabernet Franc in early vintages but I preferred 100% Cabernet Sauvignon; it is such a great variety when it is ripe that it doesn't need anything else, it's a complete variety."

The wine started out with Cabernet Sauvignon from the Montepeloso hill, but as the new plantings at the Fontanella vineyard have come on line, they have formed an increasing proportion of the blend. Whether it's because of the difference in exposure (southwest at Montepeloso as opposed to west at Fontanella) or the age of the vines (old at Montepeloso but only a few years old at Fontanella), barrel samples show a much richer wine from Montepeloso, but perhaps the blend is more complex.

Fabio is considering an old vines selection from Montepeloso (but the issue of course is the effect of taking this out of the Gabbro.) I asked about stylistic objectives and reference points? "A reference point for sure is the old style California Cabernet, Ridge Montebello or Heitz Martha's Vineyard, it goes in a direction I can see here, not as an imitation but as an expression of Cabernet. So the reference points are California Cabernets from the period when they were elegant, before they became brutal." It's ironic that Fabio's intention was (and still is) to produce a great wine from indigenous varieties, but his first great success has been with a 100% Cabernet Sauvignon, but the search for elegance continues.

Tua Rita ✱✱

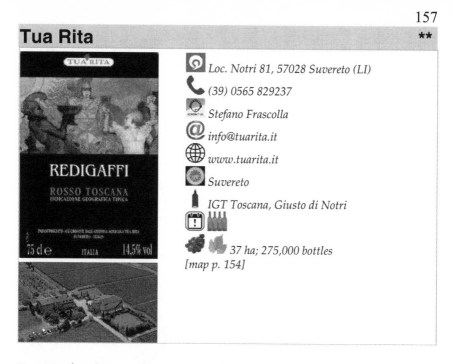

Loc. Notri 81, 57028 Suvereto (LI)

(39) 0565 829237

Stefano Frascolla

info@tuarita.it

www.tuarita.it

Suvereto

IGT Toscana, Giusto di Notri

37 ha; 275,000 bottles
[map p. 154]

Tua Rita has been a fantastic success story, reaching cult status within a few years of its first release. The estate was founded in 1984 when Rita Tua and her husband Virgilio Bisti planted Cabernet Sauvignon and Merlot in Suvereto. The vineyards are on the low-lying hills overlooking the town of Suvereto. Extended in 2002, the cellar is built underground to allow for gravity feed. The first vintage was released in 1992.

Giuso di Notri, a Bordeaux blend of Cabernet Sauvignon, Merlot, and Cabernet Franc, is the signature wine named for the first vineyard that was planted; the style Is international. Redigaffi, a 100%% Merlot whose first vintage was 1994 with only two barriques, became the cult wine by the end of the decade. Matured in new French barriques, this has a full force style. Perlato del Bosco is a monovarietal Sangiovese (until 2011 it also contained Cabernet Sauvignon). Per Sempre is a monovarietal Syrah; another Syrah, Keir, introduced with the 2016 vintage, has the novelty of aging in amphora, and has an elegant, fresh style. Rosso dei Notri is effectively a second wine from the young vines, and is a blend of all the varieties; aged in stainless steel, it's intended for easy drinking. There are also two white wines.

The second generation, in the form of daughter Simena and son-in-law Stefano Frascolla, has been running the estate since Virgilio's death in 2010. In an expansion in 2015, they rented Poggio Argentiera in Grosseto.

Mini-Profiles of Important Estates

Chianti Classico

Tenuta Di Bibbiano

*Via Bibbiano 76, 53011 Castellina
in Chianti (SI)*
(39) 0577 743065
*Tommaso & Federico Marrocchesi
Marzi*
info@bibbiano.com
www.tenutadibibbiano.it

🍇 🔥 *25 ha; 100,000 bottles*
[map p. 43]

The winery has been in the hands of the Marzi family since 1865. The estate extends over 220 ha. About half of the 25 ha of vineyards were planted in the late 1950s, the rest between 2000 and 2005. Oenologist Julio Gambelli made the wine from 1943 until Stefano Porcinai took over in 2001. Winemaking is a mix of traditional and modern. The Chianti Classico includes indigenous varieties Colorino and Canaiolo, and ages in large (25 hl) vats. The Montornello Riserva includes a little Merlot. The single vineyard Vigna del Capannino has become a Gran Selezione, made only in top vintages, and ages in a mixture of Slavonian vats and French barriques.

Castell'in Villa

Loc. Castell'in Villa, 53019 Castelnuovo Berardenga (SI)
(39) 0577 359074
Coralia Pignatelli
info@castellinvilla.com
www.castellinvilla.com

🍇 🔥 *48 ha; 120,000 bottles*
[map p. 43]

This is a historic estate, run down with only a hectare of vineyards when Coralia Pignatelli purchased it in 1967. Planting began in 1968, and the first Chianti Classico was released in 1971. The vineyard Poggio delle Rose was planted in 1990 and became the basis of a single vineyard wine from 1996. Santacroce started in 1983 as a pure Sangiovese aged in barriques, but Cabernet Sauvignon was included from 1988. Today the estate of 300 ha includes 32 ha of olive groves as well as the 54 ha of vineyards.

Castellare Di Castellina

*Loc. Castellare, 53011 Castellina in
Chianti (SI)*
(39) 0577 742903
info@castellare.it
www.castellare.it

 *33 ha; 250,000 bottles*
[map p. 43]

The estate of 80 ha is an example of polyculture, with 12 ha of olive groves and 15 ha of other agriculture, as well as the vineyards. It originated in 1968 when five farms were consolidated, and produced its first wine in 1971. It has been owned since the 1980s by Paolo Panerai. About half of production is Chianti Classico (including Riserva in the best vintages). There are about 35,000 bottles of I Sodi di San Niccolò, a super-Tuscan from Sangiovese and Malvasia, and much smaller amounts of Coniale (100% Cabernet Sauvignon), Poggio ai Merli (100% Merlot), and some white wines based on Chardonnay and/or Sauvignon Blanc.

Fattoria Castelvecchio

*Loc. San Pancrazio, via Certaldese
30, 50026 San Casciano in Val di
Pesa (FI*
Filippo Rocchi
(39) 0558 248032

On the border between Chianti Classico and Chianti Colli Fiorentini, the property dates from the medieval period, and has belonged to the Rocchi family since 1962. The 70 ha estate includes 30 ha of vineyards and 15 ha of olive groves. Renzo Rocchi built up the estate in the mid nineties, and today it is run by his children Filippo and Stefania. Just to to the west of Chianti Classico, the DOCG

info@castelvecchio.it
www.castelvecchio.it

27 ha; 120,000 bottles
[map p. 42]

wines are Chianti Colli Fiorentini. There are IGTs from international varieties, including Solo Uno (100% Cabernet Sauvignon) and Il Brecciolino (Sangiovese, Merlot, and Petit Verdot).

Famiglia Cecchi

Località Casina Dei Ponti, 53011 Castellina in Chianti (SI)
(39) 0577 54311
cecchi@cecchi.net
www.cecchi.net

 330 ha; 8,000,000 bottles
[map p. 43]

This the flagship winery in the Cecchi group. The first winery was Villa Cerna, established at the southern boundary of Chianti Classico in the 1960s, Castello Montauto in San Gimignano came in 1988, Val Delle Rose in Maremma was purchased in 1996, and Tenuta Alzatura in Umbria was added last. But Cecchi is somewhat of a catch-all name for activities of the group: wines include Brunello di Montalcino, Vino Nobile di Montepulciano and a long list from all around the area. In Chianti Classico, there are wines under the Villa Cerna label and also under Famiglia Cecchi, but no single cuvée stands out as epitomizing the house.

Castello di Gabbiano

Mercatale Val di Pesa, via Gabbiano 22, 50020 San Casciano in Val di Pesa (FI)
(39) 0558 21 053
castellogabbiano@castellogabbiano.it
www.castellogabbiano.it

145 ha; 1,000,000 bottles
[map p. 42]

The winery is located in a historic castle, and this is a very old estate, but as one of the largest producers in the region, is today very much in the modern idiom. The focus is on ripeness, and wines are aged mostly in barriques. Chianti includes the whole range, Classico, Riserva, and Gran Selezione Bellezza, (formerly a Riserva). The Alleanza IGT is a blend of Merlot and Cabernet Sauvignon.

Castelli Del Grevepesa

Via Gabbiano 34, 50026 San Casciano in Val di Pesa (FI)
(39) 0558 21101
vinoteca@castellidelgrevepesa.it
www.castellidelgrevepesa.it

[map p. 42]

The largest cooperative in the region, Grevepesa was founded in 1965 by 18 winegrowers, and now has 120 members from all over the area. Chianti Classico and Riserva are 95% Sangiovese and 5% Merlot, and are aged in botti. At the higher end, there are both Riserva (100% Sangiovese) and Gran Selezione (Sangiovese with some Merlot) from the single vineyard of Castello di Bibbione, and Gran Seleziones from Lamole and Panzano, both exclusively Sangiovese from the local areas, aged in botti. ClementeVII is a range in more modernist style, including 5% Merlot, with Chianti aged 85% in botti and 15% in barriques, the Riserva half and half, and Gran Selezione 80% botti to 20% barriques. The focus is on flavor, but without losing sight of Chianti.

I Fabbri

Via Casole 52, Loc. Lamole,
50022 Greve in Chianti (FI)
(39) 0339 4122622
Susanna Grassi
info@ifabbrichianticlassico.it
www.ifabbrichianticlassico.it

11 ha; 35,000 bottles
[map p. 42]

Istine

Loc. Istine CS, 53017 Radda in
Chianti (SI)
(39) 0577 733684
Angela Fronti
info@istine.it
www.istine.it

25 ha; 35,000 bottles
[map p. 43]

Lamole di Lamole

Via di Lamole, 50022 Greve in
Chianti (FI)
(39) 0559 331256
info@lamole.com
www.lamole.com

57 ha; 240,000 bottles
[map p. 42]

Livernano

Loc. Livernano, 53017 Radda in
Chianti (SI)
(39) 0577 738353
Martino Scheggi
info@livernano.it
www.livernano.it

25 ha; 100,000 bottles
[map p. 43]

The estate has belonged to the Grassi family since the seventeenth century. Although they began to bottle wine in the 1920s, the next two generations lost interest, and the estate was rented out. Susanna Grassi changed careers from fashion to wine when she took back the estate in 2000 and created I Fabbri. Vineyards are at elevations of 550-650m. The focus is on a local cultivar of Sangiovese: the only other variety is some Canaiolo in the Riserva. Chianti ages partly in vat and partly in 500 liter barrels: Riserva and Gran Selezione age only in 500 liter barrels of French oak. There are two IGTs: Due Donne is a equal blend of Sangiovese and Schiopetto, and Il Doccio is a monovarietal Merlot.

Angela Fronti created Istine in 1959 after starting an vineyard management company. The winery is basically a warehouse. Vineyards are in three areas, two in Radda in Chianti, and one in Gaiole in Chianti, all at altitudes around 500m. The first estate wine was produced in 2009: today there are separate bottlings from Istine (between Radda and Castellina), Casanova (near Radda), and Cavarchione (in Gaiole). The top wine is the Riserva, LeVigne. The approach is traditional, with only Sangiovese, and all wines aged in botti of Slavonian oak.

Best known for its Pinot Grigio, the Santa Margherita group owns wineries all over Italy. Purchased in 1993, Lamole di Lamole is one of three wineries in Tuscany. The historic building of the winery is now used for aging; there is a modern fermentation center in Lamole, and a visitor center at Greti in Chianti. The approach tends to be modern. Chianti Classico is light and fresh, Chianti Classico Blue Label has 20% Cabernet Sauvignon and Merlot and is rather stern, the Riserva has 5% Canaiolo and is deeper than Classico *tout court* but not as structured as Blue Label, and the Gran Selezione has 5% Cabernet and is the deepest and most modern.

Just outside Radda in Chianti, Livernano is a hamlet in a a 200 ha estate that was restored starting in 1990. It includes a boutique hotel and offers cooking classes, as well as cellar tours and tastings. There's a wide range of wines. From Chianto there's a Classico and Riserva, which contain 20% Merlot: the top Sangiovese is the IGT Purosangue. The eponymous Livernano is a Cabernet-Merlot blend. Caselvento nearby is under the same ownership: here the Chianti Classico and Riserva include 20% Cabernet Sauvignon; IGT Janus is 100% Cabernet .

Monteraponi

Loc. Monteraponi, 53017 Radda in Chianti (SI)
(39) 0577 738208
Michele Braganti
mail@monteraponi.it
www.monteraponi.it

10 ha; 50,000 bottles
[map p. 43]

The vineyards are part of a 200 ha estate, purchased by Michele Braganti's father in 1974. Vineyards were rented out, and the grapes sold off, until Michele decided to take over: his first vintage was sold in 2003. The cellars are underneath the medieval tower of the Monteraponi hamlet. Winemaking is traditional, with aging in large, old botti. The focus is on indigenous varieties. Chianti Classico and Riserva Il Campitello (from the oldest vineyard) are both Sangiovese with small amounts of Canaiolo or Colorino. Baron Ugo (named for the eleventh century owner of the village), which comes from the highest vineyard, was a Riserva until 2012, but then became an IGT to give more flexibility in production (but it has the same blend of Sangiovese, Canaiolo, and Colorino). There will soon be a 100% Sangiovese from a newly planted vineyard.

Fattoria Nittardi

Loc. Nittardi 76, 53011 Castellina in Chianti (SI)
(39) 0577 740269
Leon Femfert
info@nittardi.com
www.nittardi.com

35 ha; 100,000 bottles
[map p. 43]

The name is a contraction of Nectar Dei, the name of a fortification at the boundary between Siena and Florence in the twelfth century. The estate was owned by Michelangelo in the sixteenth century. It was purchased a revived in 1982 by Peter Femfert, a publisher from Frankfurt, and his wine Stefania Canalia, a historian from Venice. Carlo Ferrini was brought in as consulting oenologist. The entry-level Chianti Classico, Belcanto, is a blend of Sangiovese from Nittardi with Sangiovese and other varieties from a vineyard at San Quirico, farther south and lower down. Casanuovo di Nittardi is monovarietal Sangiovese from the single vineyard Vigna Doghesa, with the style moving towards the richness of Brunello. The Riserva, which includes some Merlot, is made only in top years and comes from the highest altitude vineyards. The approach is avowedly modernist, with all wines aged in 500 liter French barrels, including 30% new oak for the Riserva. Nectar Dei is a super-Tuscan from Bordeaux varieties. From an estate purchased in Maremma in 1999 there are Ad Astra (a Sangiovese-Bordeaux blend) and BEN, a Vermentino.

Borgo Salcetino

Loc. Lucarelli, 53017 Radda in Chianti (SI)
(39) 0577 733541
Tonino Livon
info@livon.it
www.livon.it

15 ha; 95,000 bottles
[map p. 43]

The Livon family have been making wine in Friuli for fifty years, expanding from their original winery to purchase two more estates, and an estate in Umbria, and then in 1996 they expanded into Chianti Classico by purchasing Salcetino. Relatively small, the estate of 30 ha is half planted to vineyards. There are three wines. The Chianti Classico and the Riserva each have 5% Canaiolo; the Chianti Classico is bottled soon after fermentation, while the Riserva ages in wood. Rossole is an IGT with 70% Sangiovese and 30% Merlot, aged in new barriques.

162

Fattoria San Giusto a Rentennano

Via San Giusto 20, 53013 Gaiole in Chianti (SI)
(39) 0577 747121
Elisabetta Martini di Cigala
info@fattoriasangiusto.it
www.fattoriasangiusto.it

30 ha; 80,000 bottles
[map p. 43]

A couple of miles away from the Castello di Brolio, this estate was a Cistercian monastery that became a fort that was destroyed in the wars of the Middle Ages. It came into the Martini di Cigala family by marriage in 1914, and since 1992 has been run by Enrico Martini di Cigala and his family. The estate extends over 160 ha. Chianti Classico and the Riserva Baròncole include a little Canaiolo; Chianti Classico is aged in barrels of mixed sizes, but the Riserva ages exclusively in barriques, including 20% new oak. The top Sangiovese is the IGT Percarlo, aged in barriques and some larger casks. La Ricolma is 100% Merlot, aged in barriques. With the extensive use of barriques, including new oak, the approach here is decidedly modernist.

Savignola Paolina

Via Petriolo 58, 50022 Greve in Chianti (FI)
(39) 055 8546036
Luzius & Manuela Caviezel
info@savignolapaolina.it
www.savignolapaolina.it

6 ha; 25,000 bottles
[map p. 42]

The Fabbri family purchased this estate, then called Savignola, in 1780; in mid twentieth century the owner of the day added her name, Paolina. The Caviezel family became majority shareholders in 2014, and vineyards and cellar have been renovated,. The focus here is on harvesting late to achieve ripeness. The Chianti Classicos have up 15% Colorino and Malvasia Nero. They are all aged in French barriques. The IGT Il Granaio is 50% Sangiovese and 30% Merlot.

Tolaini

Loc. Vallenuova, 9 di Pievasciata 28, 53019 Castelnuovo Berardenga (SI)
(39) 0577 356972
Pierluigi Tolaini
info@tolaini.it
www.tolaini.it

50 ha; 250,000 bottles
[map p. 43]

After spending fifty years building TransX Transportation in Canada, Pierluigi Tolaini (known as Louie in Canada) returned to his native Tuscany in 1999 and purchased vineyards in two locations near Castelnuova Berardenga (with a view to Siena from the highest point), Montebello and San Giovanni. The approach is modern, extending from optical sorting to get grapes of uniform ripeness, fermentation in large wood vats, and aging in barriques with new oak. The Chianti Classico is 100% Sangiovese, and the Gran Selezione is a single vineyard wine from Montebello. There is a range of different blends under IGT Toscana. Valdisanti has 75% Cabernet Sauvignon blended with 5% Cabernet Franc and 20% Sangiovese, from San Giovanni. Al Passo is 85% Sangiovese and 15% Merlot. Picconero is a blend of 65% Merlot with 35% Cabernet Franc from Montebello that is intended to compete with Bordeaux.

Val Delle Corti

Loc. La Croce 141, 53017 Radda in Chianti (SI)
(39) 0577 738215

Giorgio Bianchi moved from Milan to start this winery in 1974; his son Roberto took over in 1999. This is a very small estate, with only 4 ha of vineyards, plus 2 ha that are rented. The vineyards face east, which was a problem in the early years, but

Roberto Bianchi
info@valdellecorti.it
www.valdellecorti.it

6 ha; 30,000 bottles
[map p. 43]

Villa del Cigliano

Via Cigliano 17, 50026 San Casciano Val di Pesa (FI)
(39) 0558 20033
Niccolò Montecchi
info@villadelcigliano.it
villadelcigliano.it

25 ha; 40,000 bottles
[map p. 42]

Brunello di Montalcino

Baricci

Loc. Colombaio di Montosoli 13,
53024 Montalcino (SI)
(39) 05778 48109
baricci1955@libero.it
www.baricci.it

5 ha; 30,000 bottles
[map p. 90]

Capanna

Loc. Capanna, 53024 Montalcino
(SI)
(39) 0577 848298
Patrizio Cencioni
info@capannamontalcino.com
www.capannamontalcino.com

21 ha; 60,000 bottles
[map p. 90]

has proved beneficial during climate warming. The approach is traditional, with wines aged in large old casks. The Chianti Classico includes 5% Canaiolo; the Riserva is made only in top years, from the oldest (40-year) vines and is 100% Sangiovese. A rosé is made by saignée, and IGT Il Campino is an entry-level wine made from young Sangiovese. Lo Straniero is a Sangiovese-Merlot bland.

This old estate, where the villa dates from the fifteenth century, with a courtyard surrounding a classic Italian garden, has been in a branch of the Antinori family since 1546. The vineyards are located at the western boundary of Chianti Classico, just south of Florence. The old cellars under the villa are used for aging the wine. The Chianti Classico includes 5% Colorino, while the Riserva is 100% Sangiovese: the approach is traditional, with all aging in large old casks. There are two IGTs with international varieties: Suganella is Sangiovese, Merlot, and Cabernet Sauvignon; Nettuno is a varietal Cabernet Sauvignon.

Nello Baricci purchased this estate in 1955, and was one of the founders of the Consorzio in 1967. Now run by his son and grandson, Pietro and Federico Buffi, the estate has stayed true to its roots, with wines aged only in old botti of Slavonian oak. "We want to resist the trend (to new oak)," Nello says. Vineyards are in a top location, in 6 plots on the Montosoli hill. Until recently, the only Baricci wines were Rosso and Brunello di Montalcino, but a Riserva was introduced with the 2010 vintage.

In the northeast quadrant of Montalcino, the Capanna estate looks out over the nearby Montosoli hill. Purchased by the Cencioni family in 1957—subsequently they were among the founders of the Consorzio—it is now run by Patrizio, grandson of the founders. Vineyards are all in the local area, at elevations of 250-350m, planted with 80% Sangiovese, and some Moscato and a couple of other varieties. Wines are aged traditionally in large (10 or 30 hl) casks of Slavonian oak. "Capanna today represents one of the most traditional styles of Brunello in the area," manager Daniele says. The Rosso offers a preview of the Brunello, which follows the smooth, chocolaty style, brought to its peak in the Riserva. At a lower level, there's a Merlot Sangiovese blend, which is very Merlot-ish, under the Sant'Antimo label, and also a Pinot Grigio. From 2018, visitors can stay at the Capanna Wine Relais.

Le Chiuse

Loc.Valdicava, 53024 Montalcino (SI)
(39) 0 3381300380
Lorenzo Magnelli
info@lechiuse.com
www.lechiuse.com

 8 ha; 30,000 bottles
[map p. 90]

The estate belongs to a branch of the Biondi Santi family — Simonetta Valiani is Ferruccio Biondi Santi's great granddaughter, and the vineyards were rented to Biiondi Santi for their Riserva until Simonetta decided to make wine in 1993. Aging is traditional, in botti of 20-40 hl. The house style is quite light; the Rosso di Montalcino shows fresh red fruits and is a little reminiscent of Chianti; the Brunello moves towards black fruits, but still in a lighter style. Wines are ready to enjoy soon after release.

Tenuta Di Collosorbo

Loc. Villa A Sesta, Castelnovo Del, 53024 Montalcino (SI)
(39) 0577 835534
Giovanna Ciacci
info@collosorbo.com
www.collosorbo.com

30 ha; 160,000 bottles
[map p. 90]

Located in the south on the road from Sant'Angelo in Colle to Castelnuovo dell'Abate , this was originally part of the Tenuta de Sesta estate, which was divided in 1995, into two parts, each run by a different branch of the Ciacci family. The Rosso and Brunello age in Slavonian botti with a small proportion in French barriques; the Riserva comes from a selection of the best lots, and ages only in French oak. The interest here is really in the Brunellos, but the Sant'Antimo label, Le Due Gemme is a blend of Sangiovese with international varieties, and the Rosso is a blend of Bordeaux varieties with Syrah. Lula is an IGT Toscana blend of Sangiovese with Cabernet Sauvignon.

Costanti

Loc. Colle Al Matrichese, Via San Saloni 33, 53024 Montalcino (SI)
(39) 05778 48195
Andrea Costanti
info@costanti.it
www.costanti.it

12 ha   [map p. 90]

The Costanti family moved to Montalcino after being on the losing side in the battle for Siena in the sixteenth century. They started growing Sangiovese in the nineteenth century, producing a red wine that they called Brunello in 1865. Vineyards were planted on 10 ha of the 25 ha estate in the 1970s. Andrea Costanti, a geologist by training, took over in 1983. The wines are intended for long aging. The Rosso is aged in barriques, while the Brunello and Riserva are aged half in Slavonian botti and half in tonneaux. In the difficult vintage of 2014, the Brunello was declassified to a special cuvée, the Vermiglio Rosso.

Tenuta Fanti

Località Podere Palazzo 14, 53024 Castelnuovo dell'Abata (SI)
(39) 0577 835795
Elisa Fanti
info@tenutafanti.it
www.tenutafanti.it

50 ha; 200,000 bottles
[map p. 90]

With the vineyards lying within a 300 ha estate, close to the village of Castelnuovo dell'Abata, this is one of the larger properties in Montalcino, and a major producer of wine and olive oil. A very old family estate, it has been run by Filippo Fanti since the early seventies, joined by his daughter Elisa since 2007. The general approach is to age the wines in a mix of French tonneaux and larger casks, but the style is certainly modern across the range: The Rosso and Brunello are soft and approachable, there's a little more weight to the Vallochio Brunello (which comes from the Vallochio area), but even the Macchiarelle Riserva, which comes from the oldest vines, has that some approachability. There are also red, white, and rosé under the Sant'Antimo label.

Fattoi Ofelio e figli

Loc. Santa Restituta, 53024
Montalcino (SI)
(39) 0577848613
Leonardo Fattoi
info@fattoi.it: www.fattoi.it

10 ha; 55,000 bottles [map p. 90]

Ofelio Fattoi established this winery in the area of Santa Restituta at the end of the 1970s; today it is run by his sons Leonardo and Lamberto. In addition to 9 ha of vineyards, the 70 ha estate includes 5 ha of olive trees. Production is confined to DOCG wine, grappa, and olive oil. The Brunello and Riserva age in a mix of large casks and tonneaux.

Il Marroneto

Loc. Madonna Delle Grazie 307,
53024 Montalcino, (SI)
(39) 05778 46075
Alessandro Mori
info@ilmarroneto.it
www.ilmarroneto.it

6 ha; 30,000 bottles
[map p. 90]

The name of the property reflects its origins in a chestnut drying room near the Montosoli hillside. Giuseppe Mori, a lawyer at the time, purchased the land, planted vineyards, and converted the building into a winery. The estate has been run by his son Alessandro since 1993. The vineyards are relatively old, planted in stages between 1975 and 1984. Only Rosso and Brunello di Montalcino are produced. The style of the wine is fairly tight. All wines are aged in large oak casks. The domain is best known for its single vineyard bottling, the Madonna delle Grazie, made only in top years, which takes its name from the church by the vineyard.

Mocali di Ciacci Tiziano

Loc. Mocali, 53024 Montalcino
(SI)
(39) 0577 849485
Tiziano Ciacci
mocali1956@gmail.com
www.mocali.eu

10 ha; 180,000 bottles
[map p. 90]

Dina Ciacci created the Mocali estate, and was one of the founders of the Brunello Consorzio in 1967, but the property was in polyculture, and sold its grapes, until his grandson Tiziano took advantage of the freeze that killed the olive trees in 1985: he planted vineyards and started bottling wine with the 1990 vintage. Production at Mocali is a mix of traditional and modern: Rosso di Montalcino, Brunello, and Riserva, are all aged in large casks. Vigna delle Raunate comes from the oldest vines and ages in 350 liter barriques. The Vigna delle Raunate Riserva is produced only in top vintages and ages in 400 liter barrels. In 1996, Tiziano and his wife Alessandra revived the neighboring Poggio Nardone property, and this separately produces Rosso, Brunello, and Riserva in a more modern style, with aging including a proportion of new oak. There are also several IGT Toscanas from Mocali, consisting of blends of Sangiovese with other varieties. Production was also expanded by purchasing the Suberli estate in Maremma in 2001.

Il Paradiso di Frassina

Loc. Frassina 14, 53024 Montalcino (SI)
(39) 577839031
Federico Ricci
info@alparadisodifrassina.it
www.alparadisodifrassina.it

Located just below the Montosoli hill, the vineyard resonates with the music of Mozart. "This musical vineyard is not some silly romantic dream, but part of a long-term scientific research to see how sound waves can beneficially affect the vineyard and its vines," explains the domain. They have patented the system. The estate was founded in 2000 by Giancarlo Cignozzi, a lawyer from Milan, who had been a part owner of Carpazo from when it was founded in 1970

166

6 ha; 25,000 bottles
[map p. 90]

to its sale in 1998. Il Paradiso had been abandoned, and it took two years to renovate the buildings and replant the vineyards with Sangiovese. It goes without saying that the estate is organic. There are three cuvées. The Rosso ages in 2- and 3-year 300- and 500-liter barriques, the Brunello has 30% new oak, and the Riserva in 70% 1- and 2-year oak; the oak is a mix of barrels from 300 to 700 liters, and Slavonian botti. It's actually only the 1.5 ha Mozart Vineyard used to make the Riserva (named Fluto Magico) that has music played to it, 24/7, from 50 Bose loudspeakers. There are also loudspeakers in the cellars. I cannot say that I see an effect on the wine. The house style is quite delicate: the Rosso shows light red fruits, the Brunello is a little richer and more structured, and Fluto Magico is a little rounder and riper, but along the same lines. The estate offers tours with an explanation of the Music and Vines project, and also has accommodation. There is also a similar sized estate in Maremma, planted with 12 different varieties, that makes an IGT, called 12 Uve.

Piancornello

Loc. Piancornello, 53020 Castelnuovo Dell'Abate, Montalcino (SI)
(39) 349 599 7260
Claudio Monaci
info@piancornello.it
www.piancornello.it

10 ha; 50,000 bottles
[map p. 90]

The Peri family purchased the Piancornello vineyard in 1950, and sold the fruit until they started bottling their own Brunello in 1991. The winemaker today is Claudio Monaci, grandson of the founders. In addition to the main estate in the southeast quadrant, there are 2 ha in the Valdicava area to the north. The Brunello is a blend from both. Use of about a third new oak gives a modern impression to the wine. The Rosso is a little lighter, and the Riserva is a fraction deeper. In 2015, they bought the estate of Podere del Visciolo in Montecucco, just to the west of Montalcino. The IGT Campo della Macchia combines grapes from both estates; otherwise the wines are separate.

Podere Le Ripi

Loc. Le Ripi, 53021
Montalcino (SI)
(39) 0577 835641
info@podereleripi.it
www.podereleripi.it

12 ha; 25,000 bottles
[map p. 90]

Podere Le Ripi was Francesco Illy's first project in Montalcino, before he purchased adjacent Mastrojanni (see profile), which is now somewhat better known. Podere Le Ripi was virgin land when the first vineyard was planted in 1998. It made a stir for its "bonsai vineyard," just a tenth of a hectare, planted with vines at the extraordinary density of 62,500/ha. This was the basis for the Rosso di Montalcino in 2007. There are several Brunellos: Lupi e Sirene, and its Riserva, come from "regular" dense plantings, at 11,000 vines/hectare. Cielo d'Ulisse and Zapuntel (from the Podere Galampio vineyard on the other side of Le Ripi) come from more conventional plantings, at 4,000 vines/hectare. Little is conventional here: the cellar has been built using artisanal methods avoiding cement.

Tenuta la Poderina

Loc. Poderina, Castelnuovo
Dell'abate. 53024 Montalcino
(SI)
(39) 0577 835737
lapoderina@tenutedelcerro.it
www.saiagricola.it

 49 ha
[map p. 90]

Poggio San Polo

Loc. Podere San Polo di Poder-
novi, 53024 Montalcino (SI)
(39) 0577 835101
Riccardo Fratton
info@poggiosanpolo.com
www.poggiosanpolo.com

16 ha; 150,000 bottles
[map p. 90]

Le Ragnaie

Loc. Le Ragnaie, 53024
Montalcino (SI)
(39) 0577 848639
Riccardo Campinoti
info@leragnaie.com
www.leragnaie.com

15 ha; 80,000 bottles
[map p. 90]

Tenute del Cerro is the holding company for wine properties of Gruppo Unipol, a huge European insurance company. It has five estates, with four in Tuscany or Umbria, including the flagship property, Fattoria del Cerro, in Montepulciano, and others in Montefalco Sagrantino and Monterufoli. La Poderina is the property in Montalcino, and produces only DOC wines: Rosso, Brunello, Riserva, and Moscadello di Montalcino. Rosso and Brunello age in a mix of Slavonian botti and French barriques; the Riserva ages only in barriques. The property also offers accommodation.

The well known Valpolicella producer Allegrini purchased San Polo in 2008 together with an estate at Monteluc belonging to the same owners. San Polo now describes the combined estates. "It was biodynamic, but the vines were dying," says Marilisa Allegrini. "We started over, and have converted it to sustainable." (It has the CasaClima certification.) The San Polo home estate at Podernovi was planted in 1990, and Monteluc more recently at higher vine density. Half of the vineyards are classified for Brunello. The style is between modern and traditional. "If you ask my brother," says Marilisa, "he equates modernist with technology, but we do some modern things and some traditional things." The style is on the lighter side for Montalcino: the light red fruits and tannins of the Rosso are halfway to Brunello, the Brunello has a little more weight, but the house style of elegance, you might almost say delicacy, comes out fully in the Riserva. The Rosso comes from Podernovi and ages in second-year tonneaux, the Brunello is a blend from both vineyards and ages in new tonneaux, while the Riserva aged in mix of new and one-year tonneaux. In addition to the DOCG wines, there are two IGTs: Mezzopane is a Sangiovese-Merlot blend from Monteluc aged in barriques, and Rubio is a monovarietal Sangiovese aged for 12 months in large casks. Allegrini also own Poggio al Tesoro in Bolgheri (see profile). Carlo Ferrini is the consulting oenologist.

Le Ragnaie has vineyards in three different areas of Montalcino: most of the vineyards are in the home estate, at one of the highest points in the appellation, around 600m; the Petroso vineyard is a hectare just below the village of Montalcino; and Vigna Fornace is at Castellnovo dell'Abata in the southeast corner. The Rosso comes mostly from Petroso. The Brunello takes the classic approach of blending from all the vineyards. The Brunello V.V. comes only from the Ragnaie estate, while Brunello Fornace comes only from Castellnovo dell'Abata. All the wines are aged in 25 hl botti of Slavonian oak. There is also a Chianti Colli Senesi from the Ragnaie estate, also 100% Sangiovese, but aged in French barriques. The farm house on the Ragnaie estate offers accommodation.

Tassi

*via P Strozzi 1-3, 53024 Montal-
cino, (SI)*
(39) 05778 46147
Fabbio Tassi
info@tassimontalcino.com
www.tassimontalcino.com

(!) 血

🍇 🍇 *7 ha; 20,000 bottles*
[map p. 90]

Fabio Tassi is something of an entrepreneur, with a wine shop, the Enoteca la Fortezza, showcasing the local wines in Montalcino, a restaurant, Locanda Franci, just across the street (with accommodation above), and the winery that has his name on the edge of town. The vineyards are on a single slope in Castelnuovo dell'Abata, at the southeast. Aging policy is to increase the size of the cask going up the hierarchy, so Rosso ages in 500 liter barrels, Brunello in 700 liter barrels, and the Selezione Franci in Slavonian botti. Two IGTs have unusual blends: Colsilium is equal parts of Sangiovese, Cabernet Sauvignon, and Petit Verdot, while Aquabona is equal parts of Cabernet Sauvignon and Petit Verdot.

Terralsole

*Villa Collina d'Oro 160/a, 53024
Montalcino (SI)*
(39) 05778 35764
Mario Bollag
info@terralsole.com
www.terralsole.com

(!) 血

🍇 🍇 *12 ha; 55,000 bottles*
[map p. 90]

Mario Bollag had a chequered career until he decided to become a winemaker. He created Il Palazzi in 1982, but sold it and then established Terralsole in 1996. The Pian Bossolino Vineyard around the winery is at 420m, overlooking Castelnuvo dell'Abate. The Fonte Lattaia vineyard is located lower down, around 250,between Castelnuvo dell'Abate Sant'Angelo. The style is modern, with wines aged in 600 liter tonneaux of French oak. Intensity increases from the Rosso to the Brunello, and then to the single vineyard wines from Pian Bassolino and the rich Fonte Lattaia. Pasticcio is a full-force super-Tuscan, a blend of Cabernet Franc and Merlot with some Sangiovese.

Uccelliera

*Pod. Uccelliera 45, Fraz. Castel-
nuovo, 53020, Montalcino (SI)*
(39) 05778 35729
Andrea Cortonesi
anco@uccelliera-montalcino.it
www.uccelliera-montalcino.it

(!) 血

🍇 🚜 *6 ha; 60,000 bottles*
[map p. 90]

Andrea Cortonesi was cellarmaster at Ciacci Picolomini when he purchased his first four hectares from Ciacci in 1986. They included an old farmhouse and half a hectare of old vines. Andrea renovated the house and extended the old underground cellar. His first vintage was 1991. The style is relatively fresh, deepening going from Rosso to Brunello, and become smoother, riper, and more structured at the Riserva level. There is also an IGT, Rapace, which is a blend of Sangiovese with Merlot, and Cabernet Sauvignon. Andrea also makes small amounts of Rosso and Brunello from high altitude vineyards under the separate label of Voliero (sources have varied, but are 200m higher than Uccelliera). Like Uccelliera, the wines are vinified in traditional style in large casks of Slavonian and French oak. While Uccelliera is intended to showcase the local terroir of Castelnovo dell'Abata, Voliero is intended to demonstrate the effect of blending different high altitude vineyards.

Tenuta Argentiera

Via Aurelia 412/A, Località I Pianali, 57022 Donoratico, (LI)
(39) 0565 773176
info@argentiera.eu
www.argentiera.eu

🚜🚜 *75 ha; 450,000 bottles*
[map p. 139]

Brothers Corrado and Marcello Fratini established Tenuta Argentiera in 1999 at the southern border of the appellation in what used to be part of the Donaratico estate. Ownership changed when they sold a controlling stake in 2013 to Stanislaus Turnauer, an Austrian industrialist. Vineyards are planted with Bordeaux varieties and Syrah. The Argentiera cuvée is a classic Bordeaux blend: 40% each of Cabernet Sauvignon and Merlot, and 20% Cabernet Franc. Villa Donaratico is a second wine, not as smooth, and has 10% Petit Verdot together with the other Bordeaux varieties. At the level, of a third wine, aged in steel instead of wood, Poggio ai Ginepri is a Bordeaux blend with slightly less Cabernet Sauvignon. There is also a white blend of Vermentino and Sauvignon Blanc. The Cru series are the top wines, monovarietals including Cabernet Sauvignon, Cabernet Franc, and Merlot, each named after a member of the family.

Campo al Mare

Via del Fosso, 31, 57022 Donoratico (LI)
(39) 0558 59811
Roberto Potentini & Raffaele Orlandini
folonari@tenutefolonari.com
www.tenuteambrogioegiovannifolonari.com

25 ha; 175000 bottles   [map p. 139]

Campo al Mare is the Bolgheri winery of the Folonari family, who also own Nozzole in Chianti (see profile), La Fuga in Montalcino, and wineries in Montepulciano and Maremma. The general approach is modern, emphasizing fruit, and relying on new oak. The flagship Bolgheri is a Bordeaux blend, with 60% Merlot, 20% Cabernet Sauvignon, 15% Cabernet Franc, and 5% Petit Verdot . Under Bolgheri Superiore, Baia al Vento is 90% Merlot. Both age in 500 liter barriques, with 50% new and 50% 1-year oak for Baia al Vento. There are also a rosé and a Vermentino.

Guado al Melo

Loc. Murrotto 130/A, 57022 Castagneto Carducci (LI)
(39) 0565 763238
Annalisa Motta
info@guadoalmelo.it
www.guadoalmelo.it

20 ha; 150,000 bottles
[map p. 139]

The Scienza family have been involved in wine, with an estate in Trentino, and Michele and Annalisa Scienza bought this estate in 1998. They replanted the vineyards in 1999, and constructed a new cellar in 2005. The top wine is Atis, a blend of Cabernet Sauvignon with a small proportion of Cabernet Franc and Merlot. The first vintage was 2003, but it was not produced in 2002, 2010, or 2014 as conditions were not considered good enough. Rute is a second wine, from Cabernet Sauvignon with some Merlot, and Antillo is bland of 50% Sangiovese with Cabernet Sauvignon and Merlot. Jassarte is unusual, an IGT Toscana coming from 30 different varieties that are planted intermingled: the intention is to showcase terroir rather than variety. Like Atis, it is made only in the best years. There are also entry-level wines, Bacco in Toscana (red) and L'Airone (Vermentino).

I Luoghi

Loc. Campo al Capriolo, 201, 57022
Castagneto Carducci (LI)
(39) 0565 777379
Stefano Granata
info@iluoghi.it
www.iluoghi.it

 4 ha; 15,000 bottles
[map p. 139]

Stefano and Paola Granata created this tiny property in 2000. Stefano was an electrical engineer before he decided on a change of career to winemaking. They produce two wines: Campo al Fico, a Bolgheri Superiore providing 20% of production, which is 80% Cabernet Sauvignon and 20% Cabernet Franc; and Podere Ritorti, a Bolgheri DOC, which is 80% Cabwrnet Sauvignon blended with Cabernet Franc, Merlot, and Syrah.

Fabio Motta

Vigna al Cavaliere 61, 57022
Castagneto Carducci (LI)
(39) 0565 773041
Fabio Motta
info@mottafabio.it
www.mottafabio.it

7 ha; 23,000 bottles
[map p. 139]

After five years working at Michele Satta, his father-in-law's property, Fabio Motto established his own winery in 2009. The main vineyard. Le Pievi, is in Castagneto Carducci, and produces the Bolgheri red, a blend of half Merlot with a quarter each of Cabernet Sauvignon and Sangiovese, aged in 2- and 3-year barriques. A smaller vineyard just to the north in Le Fornacelle produces a white based on Vermentino and Viognier. Another small vineyard. Le Gonnare, purchased in 2012, has clay-rich soil, and is the source for the Bolgheri Superiore, a blend of 85% Merlot and 15% Syrah, aged in barriques with one third new oak.

Podere Sapaio

Loc. Lo Scopaio 212, 57022 Castagneto Carducci (LI)
(39) 0565 765 329
Massimo Piccin
info@sapaio.it
www.sapaio.it

25 ha; 105,000 bottles
[map p. 139]

Originally from the Veneto, a graduate who worked in the family construction business, Massimo Piccin changed career and purchased the estate in 1999; it was virgin land, and he planted the vineyards in 2000. The estate produces two wines: Sapaio is a Bolgheri Superiore from Cabernet Sauvignon, Cabernet Franc, and Petit Verdot; the second wine, Volpolo, comes from Cabernet Sauvignon, Merlot, and Petit Verdot. Carlo Ferrini is the consulting oenologue.

Suvereto

Petra

Loc. San Lorenzo Alto 131, 57028
Suvereto (LI)
(39) 0565 845308
Mario Botta
visit@petrawine.it
www.petrawine.it

100 ha; 350,000 bottles
[map p. 154]

Coming from the construction industry in the 1970s, Vittorio Moretti founded Bellavista in Franciacorta, and subsequently started other wineries, Contadi Castaldi, also in Franciacorta, and La Badiola in Maremma. Petra was founded in 1997, with a striking winery designed into the hillside by Swiss architect Mario Botta. Vittorio's oenologist daughter, Francesca, is in charge. A wide range of wines is based on Cabernet Sauvignon, Merlot, Syrah, and Sangiovese, with both blends and monovarietals. A second range of wines, the entry-level Belvento, was added in 2015.

Fattoria le Pupille

Piagge del Maiano 92/A, loc. Istia d'Ombrone, 58100 Grosseto (LI)
(39) 0564 409517
Elisabetta Geppetti
info@fattorialepupille.it
www.elisabettageppetti.com

80 ha; 500,000 bottles
[map p. 154]

This part of Maremma has always been agricultural, but Elisabetta Geppetti was a pioneer in establishing vineyards for quality wine after she took over the family winery, only 2 ha at the time, in 1985. First produced in 1987, Saffredi was one of the early super-Tuscans. Saffredi started as a pure Cabernet Sauvignon, but is now a blend of 60% Cabernet Sauvignon, 30% Merlot, and 10% Petit Verdot. Poggio Valente, another single vineyard wine, followed in 1997, and is a monovarietal Sangiovese. Other wines, including the entry-level Morellino di Scansano, are blends based on Sangiovese. The style is rich and powerful, from the Morellino's fat fruits, to Poggio Valente bursting with fruits, to Saffredi, where the impression of structure tones down the fruits a bit. The winery started in a farmhouse, but with success and expansion moved to a new winery. In 2002, the vineyards were expanded by buying the 43 ha Bozzino estate on a neighboring hill.

Index of Estates by Rating

Index of Organic and Biodynamic Estates

Index of Estates by Appellation

Istine
Lamole di Lamole
Livernano
Il Molino Di Grace
Castello Di Monsanto
Monteraponi
Montevertine
Fattoria Nittardi
Tenuta di Nozzole
Panzanello
Castello Di Querceto
Querciabella
Castello Dei Rampolla
Barone Ricasoli
Rocca Delle Macìe
Rocca di Castagnoli
Rocca di Montegrossi
Tenimenti Ruffino
Salcetino
Agricola San Felice
Fattoria San Giusto a Rentennano
Savignola Paolina
Tenuta Tignanello
Tolaini
Val Delle Corti
Castello Vicchiomaggio
Villa del Cigliano
Fattoria di Viticcio
Castello Di Volpaia
Chianti Rufina
Marchesi de Frescobaldi
IGT Toscana
Bibi Graetz
Morellino di Scansano
Fattoria le Pupille
Suvereto
Montepeloso
Petra
Tua Rita

Index of Estates by Name

Books by Benjamin Lewin MW

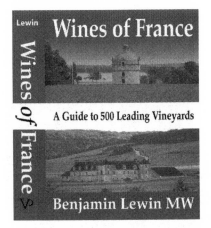

Wines of France

This comprehensive account of the vineyards and wines of France today is extensively illustrated with photographs and maps of each wine-producing area. Leading vineyards and winemakers are profiled in detail, with suggestions for wines to try and vineyards to visit.

Wine Myths and Reality

Extensively illustrated with photographs, maps, and charts, this behind-the-scenes view of winemaking reveals the truth about what goes into a bottle of wine. Its approachable and entertaining style immediately engages the reader in the wine universe.